Digital Sovereignty

Protecting Your Crypto Assets Against Common Threats

Josh McIntyre, CBP, CEP, Sec+

ISBN: 9798349335983

Dedication

For my family, both born and chosen – thank you for supporting everything I do.

For Maria, for your endless love and support throughout life – especially for encouraging my insatiable curiosity.

Acknowledgments

This book is the result of many years' work creating free and open educational content about cryptocurrencies, cybersecurity, and computer science. My passion project, chaintuts, wouldn't be what it is without the support of countless family, friends, colleagues, and viewers that have contributed their inspiration, insights, and questions.

Thank you to Jessica Levesque, my colleague and friend from the Cryptocurrency Certification Consortium (C4), for your editing expertise and positive comments on the book. Thank you to Dave Schwed, Dr. Anthony Serapiglia, and others who listened to my ideas and contributed their suggestions to the book.

Thank you to everyone that's interacted with chaintuts throughout the years – from videos, articles, code projects, talks, and more. I appreciate you tuning in and giving me the opportunity to share my passions with others.

Thank you to my family – mom, dad, John, Tian, our pets, and especially my incredible wife Maria for your endless support while working on this project. Thank you for supporting everything I do, and listening to me talk about any topic I'm fascinated by.

Part 1

Introduction to Cryptocurrency Ownership

Part 1, Chapter 1

An Introduction to Digital Sovereignty

Cryptocurrencies like Bitcoin, Ethereum, Litecoin, and many others have captured the attention of the digital world since their introduction starting in 2009. Bitcoin was first on the scene, and sparked a wave of forks, new coins, tokens, and a whole ecosystem of technologies. These coins offer self-sovereign money, a way to exchange value without relying on central authorities like governments or banks. No third party is needed to send, receive, or interact with these networks. Instead, decentralized coins use a system based on cryptography to validate transactions and verify ownership of assets.

These systems offer great power to their users – freedom from many of the restrictions and barriers in place that impede fiat transactions. There's no chargebacks for merchants to worry about – transactions are irreversible. There's no border-based restrictions for folks sending money to their family and friends across the world. While some localities may ban or restrict the use of cryptocurrencies from a legal perspective, this does not prevent a determined user from using them anyway since there is no central authority in control of the network. There's no worry about your accounts being frozen and inaccessible due to some clerical error – if you have your keys, you have your coins. *You* control your money. No one can stop you from sending a valid transaction to any other party on the network so long as you can sign that transaction with your keys. This is true digital sovereignty when it comes to money. Just you, your cryptographic keys, and a world of your peers communicating over the internet.

Decentralized currencies are undoubtedly powerful for their users in the same way the internet is as a whole. But this comes at a cost – these technologies are also powerful tools for bad actors. Scammers, malicious hackers, and thieves love cryptocurrencies, because the reward for compromising someone is an irreversible deposit in their own accounts. For this reason, malicious actors have come up with a whole industry of theft. From social engineering to technical compromise, there's a rapidly evolving world of threats that seek to separate you from your coins. In nearly all cases, there's no recourse if you get your cryptocurrency stolen – it's just gone.

For this reason, understanding cryptocurrency security is so critical for safe passage in this digital space. Peer-to-peer money means there's no central authority to trust for transactions, but it also means there's no corporate support line to call in the event of a problem. Your security is your responsibility, and yours alone. Thankfully though, you don't have to go at this truly alone. There's lots of well vetted security principles that the Bitcoin and cryptocurrency community have developed to keep your keys and coins safe.

This book is for users of every level that want to learn about digital asset security. Whether you're brand new or an expert-level user, this book will offer useful information about security practices and threats you may face as you navigate the crypto ecosystem. This book does assume some familiarity with the basics of crypto use and isn't a guide on setting up a basic wallet or sending your first transaction. But it is designed to be accessible for folks of all levels.

Most importantly, this book isn't just a collection of tips you're expected to follow because "experts" say you should. This book is about understanding the principles of security that will remain timeless as the space evolves. If you understand why a particular practice is recommended, it's easier to put into practice. We'll be discussing the basic principles of crypto asset wallets, types of wallets and security practices for them, and common threats that are out there.

This book is divided into four parts, each containing logical divisions of knowledge on crypto-security. Part 1 is an introduction to the principles behind wallets and crypto keys – a discussion of common key formats and ownership types. This section will introduce you to the ways a wallet will encode your critical private key data for backup. It will also explain the distinction between key ownership models you'll encounter – custodial and non-custodial wallets.

Once we've looked into wallet control models and private key formats, Part 2 will discuss the principles of securing custodial (often called crypto exchange) accounts. These principles may seem familiar for users of online services. We'll discuss how to create a strong passphrase, how to use 2 factor authentication, and some exchange-specific tools for enhanced security. This section will not only help with your exchange security hygiene, but can improve it for all of your important online accounts. This is a great section to share with your friends and family that aren't even interested in digital currencies.

Part 3 explains the detailed principles of securing self-custody wallets, the ultimate cryptocurrency experience. We'll talk about how to safely manage your own keys, so you don't have to trust an exchange to do so. This section covers key backups, the types of non-custodial wallets, and principles for securing each. Of particular interest to those looking to save for the long term is the section on popular hardware wallets. For everyday spending, there's a section on hot wallets too.

Finally, Part 4 will cover a fun (but perhaps scary) topic – threats. This section covers a large variety of threats I have compiled in my years as a technical educator in this space. We'll discuss common social engineering scams, malware, and even personal mistakes that can separate you from your coins. This section contains a detailed look at each threat, along with mitigation steps you can follow to prevent yourself from becoming a victim. Some threats include real-world examples from folks I have met that have lost (or nearly lost) coins.

Ultimately, this book is all about developing confidence in your ability to stay secure when using cryptocurrencies. I hope that you'll walk away with a deeper understanding of the principles that drive security. Security isn't just about applying recommended practices, although that is certainly important. Knowing *why* a practice is recommended can help you adapt to future changes in the security landscape surrounding this fast-evolving set of technologies. Self-sovereign digital asset ownership requires diligence, but it doesn't have to be confusing or scary. Knowledge builds confidence, and confident users can stand up to the threats that face them.

Part 1, Chapter 2

How Digital Asset Ownership Works

Cryptocurrency Addresses: Your Public Mailbox

At the core of interacting with cryptocurrencies is the concept of the crypto address. When making a transaction, we send coins from our wallet to the public address of another user. An address is a random string of characters generated by wallets and used to receive cryptocurrency. Cryptocurrencies, unlike traditional methods of payment such as credit cards, use a *push* model for transactions. With a credit card, you must give a private number to the merchant, authorizing them to *pull* funds from your account at the bank. But with crypto, you must get a public address from the store. Your wallet signs a transaction transferring ownership of some amount of crypto to that address.

Every transaction recorded on the blockchain is actually a digital signature, signing ownership of coins from owner to owner. Each time a transaction is made, the user must prove they are the rightful owner of coins at their address by providing this digital signature that all other parties on the network can verify. The transaction signs over ownership to the new receiving address of the other party. So, you sign over some coins to the store's address when you buy goods from them. If you pay a contractor in cryptocurrency, you sign ownership of a certain amount of coins over to their address.

The model of recording ownership varies from blockchain to blockchain. Bitcoin, Litecoin, and Bitcoin Cash use what is called a UTXO model. UTXO stands for Unspent Transaction Output. These are a collection of values that act almost like a digital version of cash, dollar bills and coins. Each UTXO is a specific amount of coins that is owned by a particular address. For example, a wallet might have outputs for 1 LTC, 0.5 LTC, and 2 LTC. If a user wishes to buy a computer, their wallet can combine all these available UTXOs into a transaction equaling 3.5 LTC and transfer it to a new UTXO owned by the merchant. You can also split UTXOs into value and change, for example using a 0.5 LTC UTXO to buy a 0.25 LTC shirt and sending the remaining 0.25 to your own wallet. A wallet handles this automatically for you; there's no need for the end user to think about UTXOs and change.

Other coins like Ethereum's native token, Ether, follow an account model, more similar to a bank ledger. Each Ethereum address has a balance, and a list of deposit and withdrawal transactions. This model is a little simpler to understand. You might have a 1 ETH balance, with a 1.5 ETH deposit at one point in time and a 0.5 ETH withdrawal at another point. This is just like looking at your bank account balance over time.

This book assumes you already have some familiarity with this process of creating cryptocurrency transactions and won't go too in depth with how these crypto transactions work. What is more important to think about in the context of security is how addresses and their underlying keys form the basis for cryptocurrency *wallets*. The address isn't randomly generated in and of itself. It is derived from an individual private key from the user's wallet.

Every crypto wallet is a collection of randomly generated private keys and their associated addresses. This core concept is key to our understanding of security, so it's worth saying again: *Every crypto wallet is a collection of randomly generated private keys and their associated addresses.*

Since private keys are ultimately used to sign over ownership to another address in a transaction, these keys are what we must protect. With non-custodial wallets, we must protect our own keys – ensuring safe backups, avoiding phishing, and using secure software. With exchange or custodial accounts, we must ensure that the accounts are secure so that nobody can make transfers to their own addresses. And always, we must keep an eye out for phishing, scams, and other social engineering attacks that ultimately want us to transfer coins to attacker addresses.

Private Keys and Seed Phrases

Before we can discuss safe and secure storage of our crypto keys, we need to understand what these cryptographic secrets look like. Having a better idea of the data our wallet contains will allow us to make informed choices about backups. We need to know the format of key data, its weaknesses and strengths, and possible storage media before figuring out how to keep it safe.

For wallets newer than around 2014, the mnemonic seed phrase is the standard all common wallets use. This standard is defined by Bitcoin Improvement Proposal 39 (BIP39). Although the standard originated with Bitcoin, it is widely adopted by other cryptocurrencies as well. Your keys will take the form of 12 to 24 English words, in a specific order. Other languages are also available, but English is the most common and likely for readers of this book. Most commonly, you'll get a seed of either 12 or 24 words from a wallet, but sizes 15, 18, and 21 are also supported by the standard. Here's an example of a randomly generated seed:

```
finish hawk expose abstract fiscal change
artwork enter party genuine taste swamp
```

Don't use this example seed phrase for anything, as any reader of this book could steal your coins! This seed is a 12 word phrase, which encodes 128 bits of randomly-generated data from the computer's secure random source, along with a cryptographic *checksum* contained in the last word. It's important to note that the mnemonic generation must use a cryptographically secure random source for generation, and that the last word includes a specially-calculated checksum based on the previous words. You cannot simply pick 12 or 24 words at random from the list to create a seed on your own – this won't work due to the checksum, and would also be insufficiently random.

The algorithm for generating a seed starts with 128 to 256 bits from a cryptographically secure source. These are built into your computer's operating system, or into the chip used on a hardware wallet. Next, the entropy is hashed using SHA-256 (a secure hashing algorithm), and a certain number of bits from that hash are added to the end of the entropy depending on the size of the seed. Finally, the entropy bits are split into chunks of 11 bits each and used to select the words from the 2048 word dictionary. 2 to the 11th power is 2048, so there's a word in the list for every possible 11 bit chunk. You don't have to understand the cryptography and computer science of bits to use a mnemonic, but it's helpful to understand the basic algorithm and therefore why you can't just pick some words out of the list to make your own seed.

These seeds make it very convenient to back up your wallet, as all you have to do is store those words in case you need them. We'll discuss how to do so securely and why this is so important in later chapters. The true power of BIP39 mnemonics comes not only from this convenient encoding, but in how this can be used to store an *entire wallet* in only 12 to 24 words. BIP39 is combined with BIP32 and BIP44 to create *hierarchical deterministic* wallets. This algorithm uses the single seed to generate infinite addresses in a predictable manner. As long as you have the seed and the appropriate derivation path for your desired wallet, you can always generate the same individual keys and addresses to restore a wallet.

BIP32 is the standard for hierarchical deterministic wallets. In practical terms, this simply means the ability to go from a seed to any number of sub-wallets, and individual private keys and addresses. BIP44 specifies a standard set of derivation paths for various cryptocurrencies, so that wallets can easily interoperate with one another. This means that if you have your seed phrase you use with a BIP44 wallet containing some Bitcoin, Ether, and Litecoin, you can import that seed into another BIP44-supporting wallet and access those coins again. Your wallet, following the standard, knows exactly how to generate the same set of addresses and individual private keys from the seed.

From the seed, a wallet ultimately derives individual private keys and addresses. In fact, before seed phrases existed, a wallet consisted of a set of completely random individual private keys. Backups were trickier then because the wallet file would continually increase in size every time a wallet "ran out" of fresh addresses in the original file. Wallets generally give the user a new address each time one is used for privacy purposes. Addresses may be reused securely; it just reduces user privacy to do so. An individual private key can be encoded in a more human readable format for backup. Bitcoin and Litecoin wallets use the Wallet Import Format (WIF) for individual keys, a base58check encoding. These may have various prefixes, and an "L" prefixed key is shown here. Ethereum uses a hexadecimal encoding common to other cryptographic keys, and keys always start with 0x.

```
L3yQrhEGMmEuqB12n5vkqXch2snrUdnJhaXizobqHBjC
2rgKoS1Z
```

An example of a Bitcoin WIF private key

```
0x04cc2c4c1b692f8c5f98fddd3ec129ac56e550882c
67589dc4f2f305fdab3bc7
```

An example of an Ethereum hex private key

Whether they originate from a seed phrase or are generated individually, private keys are used to derive public addresses. Cryptocurrencies are a fantastic example of *public-key cryptography*, where the system has both private keys, kept secret, and public keys that can be shared with anyone. The address is a hashed public key, which you can give to anyone so they can send coins to you. Addresses are not just the raw pubkey, but are a cryptographic hash of the public key with additional encoding. Nobody can take coins or spend coins using just your address. In order to spend those coins, you need the private key. This key is used to sign a transaction sending coins to someone else.

Seed Phrase - Known Only to the user:

```
winner lend lava fee wise potato judge
winner remove trial draw spray

     used to derive the
```

Private Key - Known Only to the user:

```
L3yQrhEGMmEuqB12n5vkqXch2snrUdnJhaXizobqHBjC
2rgKoS1Z
```

    used to derive the

Public Key - Known to anyone:

02cca4732adae5bae3d1679a0698d8b76af0ae2d9af1279b0848bbad0505c107ac

    used to derive the

Address (Public Key Hash) - Known to anyone: 1B8EWT74nUCBDXhvDVHiumFMvue2MoK53v

A user must *always* keep their private keys and seed phrases secret and safe. These keys can be used to sign transactions transferring coins to someone else's address, an irreversible action. Addresses can be shared publicly, and cannot be used to do anything other than send coins to you. If you are using a wallet with a seed phrase, it is important to note that you should never share your xpub (extended public key). This can be used to see all transactions for your entire wallet, not just for a single address. The xpub cannot be used to steal your coins, but it does present a privacy risk which may make you a target for other attacks. Our education and efforts around security will focus on keeping private keys safe, so that nobody can spend your coins but you.

Part 1, Chapter 3

Custodial vs. Non-Custodial Wallets

We know that private keys are the core of cryptocurrency ownership. Ultimately, whoever has the signing key can create a transaction from one wallet to another. But how exactly those keys are managed can take several different forms. The highest level distinction between wallets is that of *custodial* vs. *non-custodial*. These two vastly different strategies for key management will impact how we approach our security practices, so it's important to understand the difference.

Non-custodial or self-custody wallets are the most powerful and self-reliant form of key management. With self-custody wallets, the user holds the keys themselves. This means getting a seed phrase, wallet file, or individual private keys from the software when you create a wallet. This is the original form of a Bitcoin wallet and offers the intended power of Bitcoin – you hold your own money, and you don't have to trust anyone else to do so. Most major cryptocurrencies are decentralized, meaning no single authority has control over the network, transactions, or key ownership. Holding your own keys in a self-custody wallet means that no central institution can stop you from sending money to someone else. So long as your transaction is valid and signed, it will be accepted by the decentralized crypto network of your choice.

Non-custodial wallets offer several distinct advantages for security. The first aspect is, again, the lack of counterparty risk. This means that we don't have to trust someone else with the keys or transaction signing. This helps the decentralization of these networks. The more people that hold their own keys or run their own nodes, the less that the overall health of the network is concentrated in central places like exchanges. This also lowers the overall *attack surface* and concentration of risk for the keys themselves. An exchange holding the keys for many users provides a greater target for attackers than thousands of individual users, with keys spread out across many wallets. When holding your own keys, you're a less likely target for hackers looking to steal high-value keys.

Many individual users are still targeted through various attacks though, and an advantage of non-custodial management is that we can tailor our security practices for our individual needs, knowledge, and risk profile. When you're in charge, you can ratchet up the security to a higher level than an exchange that has to balance convenience, liquidity, and security for thousands of users. If you're using a wallet for spending money, you can still have reasonably high security by following the hot-wallet guidelines detailed later in this book. And to protect your life savings, you can plan to use a cold wallet strategy with several layers of protection.

All of this is done on your terms, based on your own individual *threat model*. Some will have a higher risk – high profile individuals in the crypto space, those with a high net worth and large amounts of cryptocurrency, or those that do frequent trading or high volume transactions. These individuals will need to craft a more careful and thorough plan with layered security. Someone holding a few dollars' worth of crypto for everyday spending will not need to follow all of the same practices to maintain a serviceable level of security.

There's one large risk with the non-custodial approach, however – us. Human beings are notoriously bad at computer security, and we all make mistakes. Depending on your individual level of learning, knowledge, and sophistication, self-custody may present more risk than benefits. It's all up to the individual's needs, desire to learn, or expertise in security matters.

The *custodial* approach keeps that issue in mind and creates essentially a wallet-as-a-service where the user doesn't have to worry about the key security explicitly. These wallets hold the keys for the users, and sign transactions internally without giving the user a copy of the secret keys. This models a more traditional banking relationship. You trust the bank to hold your balance and give you access to your money when you need it. This has the disadvantage of requiring trust, and thus removing some of the advantages that cryptocurrencies have in the first place.

We cannot discount that this approach adds significant risk – that of the exchange collapsing, having a breach of the keys, or simply blocking our access to the coins. However, there's also the advantage of security through familiarity. Having a simple password and 2FA is more familiar for many users, and eliminates the risk of making a mistake with the more complex key management needed for self-custody. Having a dedicated team of cybersecurity experts to manage your keys can be an advantage if you're not yet ready for the challenges of self-custody. Sometimes the best and most secure approach is simply the one that works, even if it's not the most "optimal." There's a certain advantage to removing user-error from the equation.

How we secure wallets of either kind will be the intense focus of this book. Regardless of your chosen path, or if you choose to use both, we'll dive into detailed security practices you can apply to your own strategy. For custodial wallets, we'll cover the details of passwords, 2FA, and extra practices that can help your security posture. For non-custodial wallets, we'll discuss the various ways in which you can keep your private keys out of the hands of would-be thieves, for every level of wealth from everyday spending to life savings. All of these will be detailed with not only the recommended practices, but *why* those practices are recommended. True understanding of how security works will help you develop a plan for your own needs instead of just following a checklist from an expert.

Part 2

Custodial Account Security

Part 2, Chapter 1

Exchange Security Basics

Given that the core of crypto asset ownership is private keys, you may wonder why we should even care about exchange security at all. After all, the end goal of digital sovereignty would likely include holding our own keys. The reality is, however, that many in the world simply want to experience the use, trading, or saving of cryptocurrencies without the time, energy, and friction involved in self-custody. While the non-custodial wallet user experience can be fairly simple and continues to improve, custodial wallets simply offer the experience closest to what folks are used to.

Crypto exchanges and custodial wallet services act similarly to a bank. They hold the actual private keys for those assets, which you (the end user) do not have access to. They take the responsibility for securing those keys against theft or exposure, while you provide them with some sort of profit – whether that comes from trading fees, paid software, or simply serving you ads. Exchanges come with *counterparty risk*, meaning basically that you have to trust them with your money just like you would a bank. While this does run counter to the "be your own bank" ethos of digital currencies, there are some distinct advantages to this approach.

For many users, the function and familiarity the custodial crypto experience provides better fits their use cases. If you're not looking to hold your own money, or simply want exposure to the price movement of digital assets, a custodial service certainly makes the process easier. Custodial wallets provide the least friction for people looking to use a wide variety of assets or conduct frequent trading. In many cases, the custodial approach serves as a sort of training or on-ramp for learning how to use digital assets, before graduating to self-custody. For even the most advanced, self-custody, self-sovereign minded users, exchanges serve as a valuable on and off ramp to trade fiat currency for digital assets. Unless you're staking or mining, you're most likely trading your local currency for crypto in order to get involved in the first place.

Regardless of what drives a user to custodial services, the big advantage in security comes with the familiarity of security procedures. An exchange account is usually set up in the same way as a social media, email, storage, or other online account. The log in flow uses passwords, two-factor authentication, an email or username, some account recovery options, and the like. This experience is vastly more familiar for most users than seed phrases, raw private keys, secure backups, wallet compatibility issues, and the idea that if you mess up there *is no recovery* in most cases.

The self-custody savvy may turn up their nose at this approach, trading the value of cryptocurrency self-sovereignty for yet another banking relationship. But sometimes the best way to be secure is to use what you already know, while you slowly build up the knowledge needed to self-custody with confidence. While many of these concepts are conceptually familiar to those enthusiastic enough to pick up this book, there are still many nuances and pitfalls with online account security. The next chapters will dive into account security concepts, especially as they apply to cryptocurrency services. Although the focus will be on protecting crypto-related accounts, these practices will apply to all sorts of online services and enhance your overall digital security posture.

First, we'll look at passwords – a common weak-link in security. We'll discuss what makes a good passphrase, how passwords can be compromised, how to securely store them, and passwordless alternatives. Next, a look at two-factor authentication (2FA) methods. What 2FA is, why it's important, and which methods provide the best security. And finally, we'll discuss some additional security steps useful for crypto exchanges and your critical linked accounts.

Part 2, Chapter 2

How Passwords Are Stored, Stolen, and Cracked

For most users of technology, passwords are a familiar part of the everyday workflow. Every time we log into our PC, visit a website, or interact with a crypto exchange, we have to enter a password to prove who we are. Despite the myriad of security problems with passwords, they are the most ubiquitous way to authenticate to digital services. Understanding password security is a key part of overall security hygiene, especially when it comes to critical services like cryptocurrency exchanges or other custodial wallets.

For most people, password choice is often misunderstood as simply picking something about you that seems "random" or unknown (a pet's name, the model of your favorite car), adding a few wing-dings to the phrase (numbers and symbols), and using that beautiful password on every service you can think of. But that simplistic approach leads to easy password theft, account compromise, and a user left wondering how the hackers got into their stuff so easily.

True password hygiene isn't necessarily complicated, but involves a lot more nuance than picking *kittycat123!* and calling it a day. Developing crack-proof password security involves understanding several components. First, understanding how software developers actually *store* passwords, and how attackers *crack* stolen password hashes (more on what a "hash" is to come).

Next, understanding what makes a password *resistant* to password cracking attacks, so that if a service's password database is compromised, attackers won't be able to figure out what your password is. And finally, what to do with the passwords on your end – understanding the importance of avoiding password reuse, and how to store your growing list of credentials.

How Passwords are Stored

Understanding password strength starts with understanding the attacks that passwords must be strong against. Knowing how passwords are stored by services and how hackers compromise those stored credentials will help us understand what makes a good password versus a poor one. Services like crypto exchanges don't simply store passwords in their raw form in a database somewhere, simply checking the one you type into the login form against the string that they have tucked away.

Imagine a service that stores everyone's password in plaintext form. When you type your password into the login form and hit "submit", the server compares your plain password to the value in the database, finds a match, and lets you in. While that may seem reasonable, there's a huge danger to users in the event of a password breach. Imagine now that a hacker gains access to the password database, and exfiltrates all of the available usernames and passwords. They now have access to everyone's account, no questions asked, with no further work required. It doesn't matter if someone's password is "abc123" or if it is a 50-character completely random, unguessable string. They have the password right there and can use it to log into your account.

For a cryptocurrency exchange, that means free unfettered access to all of your money! For a backup site, access to all of your data is now one click away. Very, very bad news for the victims of such a breach, no matter how strong their password actually was. Some very inexperienced web developers have done this, and there's a particularly amusing security-focused website called *Plaintext Offenders* that compiles a database of these instances. One well-known example in the security community is RockYou, a social media company that suffered a massive data breach of plaintext passwords in 2009. This wordlist is still used today for password cracking and education.

Instead of the plaintext password (for example, "rockyou"), security-minded developers store a special value called a *password hash.* A *hash* is a cryptographically secure one-way algorithm that takes an input and gives the same output for that given input every time. For example, one common hashing algorithm called SHA-256 always gives the same output for the input "rockyou". Represented in hexadecimal notation, (base-16), the first few characters of output read "4980b1f2". The full hash is quite a bit longer, 256 bits of information which is 64 characters of hexadecimal.

Those technical details aren't very important here, but what is important is that the same password "rockyou" gives the same output "4980b1f2" and so on every single time. Many developers use password-specific hashing algorithms that are designed to add additional data (called a salt) and run much more slowly than a general-purpose hash. This makes each cracking attempt by the attacker more expensive in terms of computational power and time and slows down attacks significantly. The Argon2 hash of "rockyou" requires an additional salt "foobarbaz" along with the passphrase, and gives us a hash value starting with "YMol" in base64 encoding.

```
rockyou →
```

```
4980b1f29fa32ff18c95d0ed931fd48e1ad43a729251
d6eddb3cece705ed4d05
```

An example password hash for "rockyou" using SHA-256

```
rockyou (with salt foobarbaz) →

$argon2i$v=19$m=16,t=2,p=1$Zm9vYmFyYmF6$YMol
jsb76DqkMZExF1AZZg
```

An example password hash for "rockyou" using Argon2

The other key detail here is that this algorithm is one-way. There's no formula for going backwards from "4980b1f2" back into "rockyou." Hashing is different from encryption because it's one way, whereas with encryption you can go backward from the garbled ciphertext into the plaintext using the key. This one-way property offers a particularly useful tool for safely storing passwords. Instead of storing the raw passwords, the service stores only the password *hash*. When a user types their plaintext password into the login form, the site then hashes that attempt and compares it to the stored hash in the database. If the hashes match, that means that the user has the correct password. If the hash is different, the user does not have the correct password and should not be authenticated.

Imagine now that an attacker gets access to our password database, but this time they don't get access to the passwords in a form they can use to log in. A password hash by itself isn't useful. Now, they can't immediately use this breached database to compromise accounts. There's another layer in the way, that of the password hashing algorithm. Again, this algorithm is one-way only, so there's no recipe a hacker can use to go backward and find the original password. The only path for an attacker to find the password input for the hash output is to guess, and guess, and guess possible passwords until a match is found.

How Hackers Crack Passwords

If hackers have a password hash, the only technique that can be used to find the original password is to guess a possible candidate, run it through the hashing algorithm, and check if the output matches. This is called password *cracking*, and can involve several techniques and barriers depending on how the passwords are stored.

Password cracking usually involves attempting passwords very rapidly, using a computer to run through the possibilities. In most cases, attackers aren't manually typing their password attempts into the website's login form, waiting for a response, and trying again. In fact, most services limit the number of attempts to prevent such a simple attack. Such a method is slow, rate-limited, and unlikely to work. In most cases, hackers use some exploit to get a copy of the password database, and thus have unlimited access to the user's password hashes. They can then run password cracking attacks against a target hash using fast hardware in the cloud, on a server, or even a laptop.

The need for password cracking in this context stems from another important property of secure cryptographic hashes, known as *preimage resistance*. All that means from a practical perspective is that the output of a hash function such as "4980b1f2" does not give any information as to what the potential input might be. There's nothing in the bits that give any sort of hint that "rockyou" is the input. As well, secure cryptographic hash functions usually have what is called the *waterfall effect* as a trait. This means that if any single bit of the input is changed, the output changes drastically. The input “rockyou1” gives a hash starting with “'b4588921”, nowhere near the output for “rockyou”.

```
rockyou →

4980b1f29fa32ff18c95d0ed931fd48e1ad43a729251
d6eddb3cece705ed4d05
```

An example password hash for “rockyou” using SHA-256

```
rockyou1 →

b45889216197d7709e6ca93a7d1e14c77da9e24ca4b3
7876baa4a2afd7dc66d2
```

An example password hash for “rockyou1” using SHA-256

This property means that truly the only avenue for finding the input is essentially random guessing. However, most user’s passwords aren’t actually that random, using common words or patterns that can be tried first before a hacker tries less likely candidates. As we learn about the methods of password cracking, we can build up defenses resistant to those types of attacks.

Hackers use several approaches to password cracking – brute force, and dictionary attacks or rainbow tables. The most naive, but most exhaustive form of password cracking is what we call *brute-forcing.* In a nutshell, this is cracking by trying *every single combination* of characters, within some reasonable limit. For example, trying all possible 8 character passwords comprising of lowercase letters, etc. This would mean trying everything from aaaaaaaa → zzzzzzzz by hashing every possible combination and checking against the hash we wish to crack.

Brute-forcing works well within certain length limits, around 8 to 10 characters in total. As the length of the password grows, it becomes simply impossible to try all combinations no matter how powerful the computer is. A professional password cracking cluster, with multiple powerful computers working together, can try all possible 8 character passwords comprising of letters, numbers, and symbols within a few hours. A consumer laptop can do so in perhaps a day or two. This means that no matter how random your 8 character password is, a brute-force cracker can find it.

Most people don't choose truly random passwords, and so *dictionary attacks* and *rainbow tables* come into play. A dictionary attack involves guessing candidates based on a predefined wordlist, often containing common dictionary words, passwords from previous data breaches and cracks, and even quotes from popular media. A dictionary attack allows hackers to find passwords much longer than a few characters, but predictable enough to crack due to the use of common English language words or phrases. A rainbow table is a sort of combination of both dictionary and brute force tactics, but instead of running the hash attempts in real time, the attacker pre-computes the hash and password combinations and stores them in a database for easy lookup.

Dictionary attacks combined with some brute-force like modifications are often the most powerful tool in an attacker's arsenal, trying words in a wordlist and adding numbers or special characters in various combinations. This is especially useful because many users will add numbers or symbols to common words in an attempt to make a stronger credential, such as

P@ssword1. The type of attack someone might use all depends on the circumstances, the hashing algorithms used, any intelligence they might have on possible candidates, and the available computing resources.

Part 2, Chapter 3

What Makes a Strong Password

Length vs Complexity

All of the technical details in the previous sections may or may not be interesting to you, depending on your desire to understand security internals. But those details aren't simply provided for the sake of technical enjoyment. Understanding how passwords are stored and cracked gives us a better understanding of how to generate a *strong* password that can thwart attackers.

When it comes to passwords, strength ultimately comes from *entropy*, or randomness. We know that a cracker must expend computational resources to guess possible passwords, with no way to predict what the password might be based on the hash. Attackers may try a brute-force approach, which involves trying every possible combination for a given space. But this only works for short passwords, up to around 10 characters. A dictionary attack will try possible phrases from a wordlist and variations on them. In either case, *entropy* works in our favor. The more randomness our password contains, the better.

The first key to understanding strong passwords is the relationship of password *length* and *complexity* to overall password strength. These factors can contribute to the overall entropy of the password, but in and of themselves don't necessarily indicate strength. Password complexity, in practical terms, refers to the range of characters available for creating password combinations. For example, lowercase letters, uppercase letters, numbers, and symbols. A password with letters, numbers, and symbols is more complex than a password with only lowercase letters. Length is rather self-explanatory, referring to the total number of characters in the password. A 20 character password is longer than an 8 character password, which we'll see can make a significant difference in the password's security.

Entropy is the overall goal, but in general, users should prefer password length over pure complexity. When passwords are long, additional complexity can help. But length matters far more for increasing overall entropy in the average case. This is due to the simple math involved in calculating the overall possible combinations. Don't worry, we won't be talking about difficult math here!

The possible combinations for a password of a given length and complexity can be expressed as c^l, where c is complexity and l is length. For example, let's say we'll use only uppercase and lowercase letters for our password, giving a total complexity of 52 characters. Now let's say we choose a password of 16 characters in length. That means that the total possible combinations for our passphrase is 52^{16} = 2.85e+27. That's a *lot* of guesses for an attacker to compute. In fact, this is completely impractical for even professional password cracking clusters to brute force. Let's assume 180 billion guesses per second, referred to as GigaHashes/second in computer nomenclature, from a 25 GPU cluster. In order to brute-force all possible combinations, our cracker would take approximately 503 million years to exhaust all possibilities. Even considering the world's best supercomputers dedicated to such a task, it's simply too many combinations to get through in a reasonable amount of time.

Contrast this with a password that's short but complex. Let's say our passphrase will use a combination of upper and lowercase letters, numbers, and a variety of symbols for a total complexity of 92 characters. We'll choose a length of 8, giving us a total combination space of 92^8 = 5.13e+15. Given that same cracking cluster at 180 GH/s, it would take just 8 hours (7.92 to be more precise) to exhaust every possibility.

This stark contrast in cracking time demonstrates the power of exponential increases. Because our calculation is c^l, length will always factor in much more heavily. The exponent matters more than the base. Sorry to bring math into this security focused book, but understanding this gives us a powerful tool for picking stronger passwords. Many people hold the misconception that complexity is the most important; that adding symbols, numbers, and variety in the characters used will offer the most strength. But modern password cracking attacks render those additions largely useless for any password that's too short.

Recommendation #1: Choose Long Passphrases

Given all of this information on length vs. complexity, the first recommendation is to choose long *passphrases* over a short password. If generating your own passphrases, select sentences built from multiple words that are hopefully fairly unpredictable. For example, choosing a passphrase for your exchange account, something like **ThisWhereIKeepMyMonay** would be a fairly strong choice. This passphrase, while it does contain common English words, consists of 21 characters. Such a passphrase would be completely resistant to brute-force attacks, but slightly more vulnerable to dictionary-based attacks. **ThisWhereIKeepMyMonay** is far stronger than, for example, **B@nk1nG**, even though the latter contains symbols and numbers while the former contains only English words. Modern brute-force and dictionary attacks factor in simple substitutions like @ for a, 1 for i, and so on, so they don't add value.

Overall Entropy

While length is more important than complexity in most cases, the overall *entropy* of the passphrase is what we want to focus on. Ultimately, we are aiming for a password that is hard for an attacker to guess, whether it is by brute-force or a dictionary-based attack. Remember, professional attackers can easily try 180 billion possible passwords in *one second*. A "budget" hacker with a home laptop could still try something like 7 billion per second. Every bit of entropy in our favor counts.

Human beings are notoriously bad at entropy, even though we think we are good at it. We think that coming up with a phrase like **SillyMonkeyHat** is being random, when really it's just us being a little silly for fun. Real entropy is a non-trivial problem in computer science and for human beings to comprehend.

Recommendation #2 – Generate Passwords from a Secure Random Source

A *randomly generated* passphrase offers the strongest level of security. Password manager software, or other secure password generators, can use the computer's cryptographically secure random number generator to fetch entropy, and translate it into a passphrase given certain constraints.

For example, let's say you want to generate a password for a website that contains uppercase and lowercase letters and numbers, but special characters are not permitted. A 20 character random passphrase offers a high degree of security against brute-force and dictionary attacks. Our password generator may spit out a password like **KZEEldaGkeOnYm9H4coe**. This passphrase is not only sufficiently long to thwart even the most powerful brute-force cracking computers, it's sufficiently complex and high entropy to resist dictionary attacks. There's nothing in this password that an attacker can predict, or make a reasonable guess at. No book quotes, no common words, just pure random garbage – exactly what we want.

Sometimes though, we need a passphrase that's easy for a human to type and remember – but also built from a secure random source. Enter *diceware*, an interesting technique for generating high entropy passwords that are memorable, easy to type, and consisting of English words. This technique uses a predetermined dictionary of words in a certain order, so that words can be selected by an index in the list. For example, one wordlist called Heartsucker contains 8192 words, and the Bitcoin BIP39 list

2048. These odd numbers actually have a reason behind them – the binary number system used in computing.

Each word in the list has an index from 0 - <max words>, or indexes specifically mapped to a number of dice rolls (for example 11111 to 66666). We then generate some entropy from a good random source – either from a computer's cryptographically secure source, or literal rolling of dice. We could roll a 4 or 8 sided die for binary numbers, or a common six sided die if our list is set up with the right indexes. In any case, we take that entropy and use it to select the appropriate word from our list. The more entropy, the more words. For the binary-number aware, the strange sizes of the diceware wordlists start to make more sense. 2048 words is 2^{11}, meaning each word is generated from 11 bits of entropy. 8192 is 13 bits per word. The more entropy and words we use, the more resistant our password is to cracking.

A diceware password might look something like **BawdyPatWebsterGravy**. This passphrase is generated using the 8192 word Heartsucker list, with each word selected via 13 bits of entropy. The total entropy of 52 bits is reasonably resistant to most password cracking. There's again no book quotes or popular media phrases for an attacker to try here. Even though the words are common ones, they are generated from a secure random source rather than poor human-based entropy. We're simply *encoding* secure entropy using words, not thinking up words on our own.

Thinking of Overall Entropy

Combining all these techniques and bits of knowledge together, we get a better idea of a sliding scale of security when it comes to passwords. Estimating the overall security of a passphrase is a difficult business, but there's some general guidelines we can think of when evaluating password security.

First, avoid short passwords, even with complexity substitutions like symbols. Adding an ! symbol in place of a 1 does nothing to slow down modern password crackers. Next, try to add length to your password if you're generating it yourself. A sentence is much better than two words, the longer the better. But ideally, generate a truly random password from a secure source. Password managers or other software can generate a random string with your given constraints. If you must have a password that's memorable or easy to type, use diceware software or physical dice to generate an English phrase that's high entropy.

In the end, our hierarchy of passwords looks something like this:

Bad: **B@nk1nG**
Better: **ThisWhereIKeepMyMonay**
Best: **KZEEldaGkeOnYm9H4coe**
Best: **BawdyPatWebsterGravy**

Passwordless Authentication

The best way around the security challenges of passwords is to avoid using them altogether. Due to the security risks of passwords, many technology services are moving away from them entirely and instead using *passwordless* authentication. One such example is *passkeys* – which use public key cryptography similar to Bitcoin for authentication instead of a known phrase. Passkeys can be set up with a growing number of websites and services, and eliminate much of the hassle of generating and storing strong passphrases.

When you create a passkey, your device generates a private and public key pair – similar to a Bitcoin address. The public key is stored by the website or service. Your device retains the private key. When you authenticate to the service, your device uses the private key to sign a challenge. The website can validate that signature using your public key, without having to know your private key at all. You can store your passkeys in a password manager like OnePassword, authenticator apps like Microsoft Authenticator, or even using hardware tokens like the Yubikey. This workflow is not only simpler for the end user, but it is also more secure.

Part 2, Chapter 4

Password Management and Storage

Avoiding Password Reuse

Selecting strong individual passphrases for a given service gives us better security for that site, preventing compromise in the event an attacker tries to guess your password or the service's database is breached. But individual selection is only part of our overall security posture in the broad web of digital services we may engage with. We must think about how to manage all of our credentials together, and how multiple credentials and services may interact with one another in the event of a breach.

Picking one strong passphrase to use everywhere, unfortunately, isn't sufficient. It is true that by choosing a long, strong, high entropy passphrase that we reduce our likelihood of the actual password being revealed in a database breach and password cracking attack. But that isn't the only password-leaking factor involved. Take phishing for example. There's a possibility we may be tricked into revealing our plaintext password via a phishing email or a malicious website. It doesn't matter how strong the password is, or how resistant it is to password cracking. If we simply give the attacker the password, none of that matters.

There's also the possibility that the password is cracked in a data breach and password cracking attack because we are forced to generate a relatively weak password. Some websites, although foolishly, may limit the length of the password or prohibit symbols, making brute force and dictionary attacks more feasible.

There is even the unfortunate possibility of a website storing passwords in plaintext, meaning that attackers get the raw passwords automatically if they can breach the database.

With all of these factors, it is critical on our part to limit the blast radius of such a leak. If an attacker, through whatever means, manages to get our password for one particular service, we want them to only be able to compromise *that single service*. Avoiding password reuse means choosing a strong, *unique* passphrase for every site that requires one. This adds some complexity and inconvenience for end users, but greatly increases security.

Imagine a scenario where you use the same password for everything online. You use this password for your local electric company's online bill pay. You also use this same password for your Coinbase account and your Google account. Neither Coinbase or Google is likely to suffer a data breach, as they are high profile services with deep security expertise behind them. But the electric company just laid off their IT guy and nobody has bothered to patch the out-of-date software behind their online bill pay. Not only that, but this software was written in 1990 before anyone thought better of storing plaintext passwords, so your credentials are sitting in that database in raw form. The electric company suffers a breach, and soon your password is out there for cyber criminals to exploit.

Attackers can then conduct a *password spraying* attack, using this known password from a breach associated with your name to try logging into Coinbase and your Google Mail. Since you've reused this strong, random password across services, they can now take over your account regardless of this phrase's strength. It doesn't matter that you had a strong passphrase, or that Coinbase itself was not attacked. All that matters is that your reused credentials were available for an attacker to exploit. Thus, why it is of high importance to avoid password reuse.

Password Storage

There's a problem with this method of using unique passwords for every service, though – a problem of convenience and human memory. If you are following the practices laid out in prior chapters and generating long, strong, random passphrases, you may not even be able to remember one, let alone hundreds across all the online services you use. Human beings are bad at memory as much as they are bad at entropy. So, we need a method of remembering all of these unique credentials that's convenient but also secure.

Password manager software gives us a great tool for doing so. A password manager is a piece of software designed specifically for generating, storing, copying, and even autofilling credentials. This software encrypts all of your secrets in a vault using a long, strong *master passphrase*. This means you only have to remember one strong passphrase, the one protecting your vault. The rest of your passwords can be auto-filled when you visit a website, or even copy pasted or read and typed as necessary. This tool allows you to avoid reuse, while fixing the problem of having to remember all of those great passwords. Many even have built-in password generation tools for creating strong credentials, and can store strong non-password credentials like passkeys.

Password managers come in a variety of flavors. Some are cloud based, such as the commercial 1Password or Bitwarden options. LastPass is another option that had some popularity, but unfortunately suffered a data breach that wasn't particularly well handled. There's also offline, open source managers like KeePass that offer a tighter-secured variation for those looking to avoid the cloud. In either case, these managers don't know anything about your credentials inside the vault. All encryption is done client-side using your master passphrase, and the encrypted contents are stored locally and optionally on their servers.

The downside of password managers is that they do in fact result in a central failure point. If you accidentally give up your master passphrase in a phishing attack, anyone could decrypt the contents of your vault. If your cloud-based manager suffers a breach like the LastPass breach and the attackers get a copy of your encrypted vault, they have unlimited attempts to try and crack it open using password-cracking techniques. It's absolutely critical that your master passphrase be long, strong, and difficult to crack even with vast resources and unlimited time. The theft of the encrypted vault should be part of your threat model when you choose to use a manager.

Staying aware of such breaches can give you time to rotate your passwords to new ones should such a compromise occur. After the LastPass breach, some cryptocurrency users that stored hot wallet seed phrases in their vaults noticed the theft of their assets. Their master passphrases weren't strong enough, and attackers were able to decrypt the stolen vaults to access all of their secrets. Once an attacker has your seed phrase, they can use it to sweep all of your coins and tokens to their own wallets.

For the vast majority of users, password managers are well worth the risk of having a central failure point, crypto users included. You're far more likely to have a weak or reused password used to compromise your account than you are to have your password manager attacked. It's simply a matter of exposure. While you must be aware of the risks of using a password manager, you're far less vulnerable than you are by using poor-entropy passwords that are reused all over the web. If you choose a very long, strong master passphrase and use a reputable password manager, the benefits of having stronger passphrases everywhere will far outweigh the risks of using such software.

If you're reading this book, you're probably tech savvy enough to use a password manager. That said, some folks in your life may not be. The classic, hand-written password book stored at home in a secure place isn't the worst idea either. Of course, this means that someone who steals your password book has all your passwords. Don't leave this book in an obvious place or bring it out in public. For most everyday people, physical theft of a password book isn't a likely part of your threat model. If you're a higher profile person in the crypto space or life in general, perhaps it is, and you're better suited to use a password manager and enable full encryption on all of your devices. Such physical threats are outside the scope of this work.

Part 2, Chapter 5

Two-Factor Authentication

For most online services, passwords are the first line of defense against compromise. We've learned to strengthen our passwords significantly – using high entropy, unique passphrases for all services. As noted in previous chapters, attackers still steal passphrases through a variety of means that aren't always within our control. Bad password storage happens, breaches happen, and phishing can defeat all of us. What we need next is a second layer of defense against compromise, a second *factor* that an attacker must have in order to take over our accounts. Additional layers of security come to our aid when one layer fails.

Two-Factor Authentication, often abbreviated as *2FA*, is built upon this idea of security in layers. 2FA most often means that in order to authenticate to a service, we must present two pieces of identity information that prove we are who we say we are. The most common flow is to provide both something you *have*, and something you *know*. Passphrases are something that you know. The idea is that only you should know your passphrase, giving one layer of identity verification by providing this secret. A two-factor authentication code is something that you have, a secret piece of information most often in the form of a rotating one-time code that is generated from a shared secret. Two-factor authentication is a form of multi-factor authentication. There can be extra layers added on for additional security, such as biometric factors or an additional email verification. Two-factor is simply the most common form of multi-factor as it balances convenience with additional security.

Let's say you wish to log into your crypto exchange account and have app-based 2FA enabled. When you navigate to "exchange.com/login," you are first greeted with a username and password field. You enter the thing that you know in the form of your passphrase. Once the server validates your passphrase, you are greeted with a prompt to enter your 2FA code. You open up an authenticator app on your mobile device and type the 6 digit one-time code into the prompt. The ritual complete, and all factors validated, you're allowed into your exchange account's homepage.

This workflow is fairly straightforward and adds little time for a legitimate user. But let's imagine a hypothetical attacker's attempt to compromise this same exchange account. You receive an urgent email in your inbox claiming you must verify suspicious transactions from your exchange account or it will be locked within twenty-four hours. You're busy at work, tinkering with a project, or reading. In your haste to get back to what you're doing, you follow the link in that email and enter your username and password in the form. The site thanks you for validating your account and you go back to your business. But in actuality, you've just given your passphrase to a phishing scam.

This hacker navigates to "exchange.com" armed with your freshly stolen password, or perhaps even uses a fancy script to try and log in. But instead of being granted immediate access using your password, they are greeted with the same 2FA prompt for a code they simply don't have. Thwarted by 2FA, they leave empty handed. In this scenario, this second factor prevented us from losing a valuable exchange account to a thief. There are several types of two-factor authentication, each with their own strengths and weaknesses to keep in mind. Configuring strong 2FA can protect our accounts from compromise when passwords fail.

Part 2, Chapter 6

Types of Two-Factor Authentication

2FA comes in many flavors, putting the multi in multi-factor auth. There's many possibilities from one-time codes to biometric factors such as fingerprints. But most services offer 2FA in three core configurations which we will cover here. These varieties are the ones you'll most likely see when setting up multi-factor for your cryptocurrency exchange accounts and other important services. First, SMS text message and email-based. Next, authenticator app based. And finally, hardware or security-key based MFA. All of these common forms have strengths and weaknesses, and some offer higher security than others.

Choosing the strongest form of 2FA available will greatly increase the security of our crypto exchange and custodial wallets, but we must also factor in convenience and understanding when making a selection. Much like password selection, our final decision will take into account the possible threats, our necessary level of security, and our own needs for convenience and understanding.

SMS Text Message and Email-Based 2FA

The most common form of multi-factor authentication users will encounter is SMS text-message or email-based. This form uses varying channels to send a user a server-generated one-time code that they will provide to the service as part of the login workflow. For example, you may have your phone number set up for an exchange. After entering your password correctly, the exchange's servers send a text message to your phone with a one-time password (OTP) that expires within 10 minutes or so. You enter that code into the form and are granted access. It works much the same for email, meaning you'll receive that OTP in a mail message instead of a text.

This method relies on the assumption that you and you alone have access to your phone number or email. This account, and the ability to read messages, serves as "something you have" while your password is the "something you know." So long as you retain access to your phone number and email, you'll have access to your 2FA codes. You must also ensure these accounts are secure, with strong passwords and 2FA settings of their own.

There's some problems with this assumption that only you have access to your email and phone number, though. Text messages and email just aren't the most secure mediums of communication in the first place. Neither are natively encrypted and are prone to interception as they travel across networks. As well, both are vulnerable to possible account takeover. If an attacker manages to gain access to your account at the phone company or log into your email, they can also steal your crypto exchange accounts.

Such is the reality of a common attack against SMS-based 2FA, the *sim swap.* In this attack, a hacker knows your phone number from something like a simple data breach. Perhaps the attacker even knows that you are associated with cryptocurrency. This attacker uses social engineering techniques to steal your phone number. They call the phone company's support services, pretending to be you. Perhaps saying that you lost or broke your phone and need to port or transfer the number to a new device.

This is a common thing that happens, after all – people buy new phones all the time for various reasons. The support representative, happy to assist, ports the number over to the attacker's device thinking that they are the legitimate account holder.

By simply pretending to be you via convincing social engineering skills, the hacker now has the ability to receive text messages under your phone number. They navigate to your exchange account login, hit "forgot password", and receive a 2FA code to your phone number to "verify" their identity as you. They can now take over the account and steal your funds. This scary attack has happened to many in the cryptocurrency world, especially high-profile individuals. A similar attack could occur if you forget to secure your email as highly as you do your exchange accounts. Having your email compromised often means that an attacker can reset passwords on other accounts, because the email is used to verify your identity in that case.

For these reasons, SMS and email are the weakest forms of 2 factor authentication. They work, and you will see them often. But if you can avoid them in favor of stronger methods, you should. If you can't, consider adding additional protections to your phone and email accounts. Some providers now offer sim-swap protection features, where you must provide a special PIN in order to have your number ported to a new phone. And of course, choose strong passphrases and 2FA to protect your email login.

Authenticator Application-Based 2FA (TOTP)

A better form of 2FA makes use of the ubiquity of mobile phones, minus the vulnerabilities of SMS text messages. Authenticator application (auth-app-based) 2FA is probably the most common form of strong multi-factor and is thankfully straightforward to use. This form of MFA requires the installation of an authenticator app, a special piece of software that generates one-time passwords. These apps are most commonly installed on mobile phones, but can also work on a desktop PC. The protocol is portable and does not rely on a phone number or receiving messages to work.

This model uses a shared secret and time to generate secure one-time passwords. To set up an account for 2FA, a user is provided with the secret which they import into the app. Most often, this is transmitted by simply scanning a QR code with the app, making setup less technical and error prone. The auth app then starts generating rotating one-time passwords, usually on a 30 second interval. The website prompts for one of these on setup to confirm your app is generating them correctly. Examples of authenticator apps include Microsoft Authenticator, Google Authenticator, and Duo.

Once app-based 2FA is enabled, the workflow is similar to other forms of 2FA like SMS. You enter your password and are then prompted for the 2FA code. You open up your phone and enter the rotating 6 digit code generated by your auth app, which the server can then validate. You do not have to receive a text message, instead relying on the app generating the code via the shared secret.

The most common protocol for this is called time-based one-time password (TOTP). Both your mobile phone and the server have a copy of the shared secret, the "something you have" in our authentication scheme. Both parties use cryptography to generate codes by running the shared secret and the counter (rounded for 30-second time increments) through an algorithm called a hash-based message authentication code (HMAC). The combination of the shared secret and the current time (within 30 seconds or so) means that both the auth app and the server should generate the *same* one-time password at authentication time. The fact that you can generate the same OTP as the server within a given timeframe means that you must have access to the shared secret that you received during setup. So, the server can reasonably believe that you are in fact the authorized owner of the account. If you didn't have the correct secret, your codes would not match, and the server would reject your request.

This method of authentication is much more secure than SMS or email-based 2FA, because no messages are transmitted over insecure channels. There's no worry that someone can port over your phone number (a sim-swap) and intercept codes. Provided that your clock is reasonably up to date, you can even generate codes if your phone has no network connection. The algorithm is agnostic to device or available networks.

Any compromise of TOTP 2FA would require an attacker to steal the shared secret, so that they can generate valid codes for your account. That's not an impossible task, but it's highly unlikely. A properly written authenticator app will store these secrets in an encrypted form, much like a password manager. If your device is compromised in some way, an attacker could steal your 2FA codes or shared secrets. The most likely avenue for losing 2FA codes is via phishing, where a hacker tricks you into giving them the code directly or installing remote-access software on your device.

Auth app 2FA provides a great balance of security and convenience for most users. These applications are simple to configure and use. Setup requires scanning a QR code, which most phone users are familiar with. Users can easily view and type 6 digit numeric authentication codes for login. And the fact that shared secrets are used to generate codes instead of transmitting them across insecure networks means a much smaller attack surface. You're far less likely to have malicious code running on your phone that could steal shared secrets, and even less likely to have a poorly implemented auth app leak those secrets outside of an encrypted vault. It's far easier for an attacker to execute a sim-swap attack on some unfortunately overworked phone company support agent, or to phish your email password.

Hardware-Based 2FA (U2F)

A third, even higher security option for two-factor authentication is the hardware token. Rather than a software-based app, this option uses a special-purpose device for signing authentication requests. Companies sell special devices for this purpose, and some cryptocurrency hardware wallets also feature hardware 2FA capability. This type of authentication solves some of the problems that even fairly secure app-based mechanisms have. Like app-based protocols, hardware tokens don't require network connectivity and use standard, widely implemented algorithms for ease of use and well-audited security.

Instead of scanning a QR code to enable 2FA, this mechanism asks you to register your specific device to your account. When setting up, a user is asked to insert their device into their PC's USB port and tap the device's button, or even use NFC (Near Field Communication) if setting up an account on a mobile phone. This process stores information about the device on the company's servers, but none of that information involves a private secret. In case you lose your primary device or it malfunctions, it is generally recommended to register a backup device to the account as well. These devices are generally inexpensive, and the cost is worth the extra security for valuable digital accounts. Examples include the popular Yubikey devices, and even cryptocurrency hardware wallets such as Trezor, Ledger, and KeepKey can double as hardware keys.

The most popular protocol for hardware security keys is U2F, or Universal 2nd Factor. This protocol uses public-key cryptography similar to that used for cryptocurrency transaction signing. These devices come with a private key preinstalled. When you register a device with a website, the device generates a unique private-public key pair for that website and registers the public key with the site. During authentication, you enter your password as normal and are then prompted to tap your security key. Internally, the website sends a "challenge" to the device which it must sign using the website-specific private key. The server can then verify using the public key that the signature is valid. Only the owner of the actual hardware token, and therefore private key, can generate a valid digital signature for the given public key.

Due to the fact that an attacker would have to physically steal your hardware token to gain access to an account, this method offers the highest level of security. These devices are designed in such a way that the private key cannot be extracted or duplicated, so the only mechanism for getting access to that signing key is physical theft. For the vast majority of crypto users, such theft isn't part of a reasonable threat model. Even for those that might be targeted for such theft, this is a higher barrier for a hacker than compromising app-based 2FA.

Choosing the Right 2FA for You

When choosing a suitable method of 2FA for our accounts, we must consider several factors – the level of security, the level of convenience, and our own understanding of these factors. First, it's best to choose the highest level of security available to you if possible. Using security keys or app-based 2FA if they are offered will greatly decrease your risk of account compromise. These methods are secure and have little vulnerability an attacker can leverage. Avoid SMS or email 2FA unless it is the only option available to you, or a service requires it.

Convenience and understanding must also factor into your decision, as 2FA is only helpful if you'll actually use it correctly. If you use app-based 2FA, you must consider backups. Most sites will give you a list of backup codes you can use for login in the event you lose your device or lose access to the configured shared secrets. You must safeguard these and have them available so that if you do lose your auth app access, you can still log into the account and configure a new one. With hardware tokens, you must have a backup option available, safeguard both devices, and have the device on your person every time you need to login.

The convenience tradeoff is well worth the extra security in my opinion, but that may not be true for every user. Some may find that they don't fully understand auth apps and backup codes, and may risk being locked out of a critical account if they make a mistake. Some may worry about losing access to a hardware key or backups or not wish to carry such a device with them all the time. These factors can cause users to make mistakes that might end with them being locked out of a crypto exchange account when they need their money. It's best to educate yourself on security practices like strong 2FA and make them a habit, but it is valuable to consider the tradeoffs when making those decisions.

SMS-based 2FA should generally be avoided if at all possible. The risk of sim-swaps remains a prevalent threat in the cryptocurrency community, as this is an easy social-engineering target for attackers. It is unfortunately easy to trick an overworked or panicked phone company support agent into porting a phone number, and their job is to make their customers (even the fake ones) happy. Some services sadly require a phone number as a backup 2FA method, or as a method for password resets. In that case, consider adding port-protection to your telecom account if it is available. Make sure your email is also protected by a long, strong, high entropy passphrase and strong 2FA so that attackers can't use your mail account to move laterally to an exchange.

Just as you learn to generate strong passphrases and store them securely, it's best to make 2FA education part of your security plan for crypto assets. Strong 2FA can make the difference between a frustrated attacker and a rich one if you slip up with your passwords. Mistakes happen, and without strong 2FA, all it takes is one phishing form to take your password, your exchange account, and all the coins you have stored in there. If you do have strong 2FA, you have precious time to change your passwords and re-secure your account in the event of a mistake.

Part 2, Chapter 7

Additional Exchange Security Tips

Password and two-factor authentication hygiene tend to be the most critical factors in preventing exchange account compromise. Strong passphrases, stored in a password manager, with strong 2FA will prevent the vast majority of attacks. Phishing awareness will also prevent attacks that simply try to trick us into giving up those first and second factors. That said, there are some other tools that may help us in the event of some sort of exchange account compromise, and tools that can help prevent such an occurrence in the first place. We'll discuss these strategies during this chapter. First, we'll look at how securing our email and phone number as strongly as we do our exchange accounts can prevent compromise before it happens, and advanced exchange features like address allowlisting can prevent the loss of funds after one occurs. Next, we'll discuss keeping our software hygiene up to standard – in this case focusing on our web browser.

Email and Phone Security

Now that we understand passphrase and 2FA hygiene, the first step is to of course apply these skills to our critical exchange accounts. Go to Coinbase or Gemini or Binance with a unique, high entropy password, and store that in a secure password manager. Next, buy a Yubikey security device and enable that, with strong app-based 2FA as a backup. All of those are excellent practices, but we must not forget something else associated with that account – our email, and perhaps our phone number.

For most online accounts, including cryptocurrency exchanges, an *email address* is associated with it. Often, the email serves as the username itself. This serves a purpose for online service providers – it gives them an instantly accessible means of communicating with their users. You may receive emails about promotions, changes to services, or even security issues. But this public email-as-username system comes with a bit of a flaw, in that it gives attackers a juicy, perhaps less well-protected target.

In most cases, websites have a “forgot password” feature in case a user loses their credentials. The user receives an email with a password reset link, allowing them to set a new credential and regain access to the account. Sometimes, this will also involve entering 2FA codes or tapping a security key, which does enhance security. But in many cases, all a user needs to reset their password is access to that email account.

The service rightly assumes that only the legitimate user should have access to their email, so it serves as an alternative identity verification checkpoint for access to the site in the event a password is lost. But attackers can exploit this by compromising the *email*, instead of directly compromising the exchange. Let’s say for example that after reading about password practices, you significantly upgrade your Coinbase account’s security. You’ve got an uncrackable password stored in a password manager, as described previously. But your old email account is still using that same old reused, data-breach-leaked password and no 2FA. A hacker tries a password-spraying attack on your email and gains access. In your mailbox, they see that you’re a Coinbase user, so they immediately navigate to the site, initiate a password reset, and use email access to reset your exchange password to their credential. They then clean out your account.

Good services like Coinbase will tie 2FA to the password reset process, so by enabling that you will prevent this type of attack. But the point still stands that an insecure email or phone number can compromise *one* link in the multi-factor authentication chain, and doing so may enable them to compromise other parts of the chain down the line.

We want to avoid *any* weak links in the way we authenticate to these services. So, we must give our email account the same level of security as the exchange account itself. Generate a long, strong, unique passphrase for your email, and keep it somewhere safe such as a secure password manager. Enable strong multi-factor authentication on that account, such as an authenticator app or a hardware security key. Don't forget your phone number either – enable a port-protection PIN if your provider offers it, so that sim-swaps can't be used to take over your exchange account. Treat your email and phone accounts as if they have large amounts of money in them, just as your exchange account does. Losing your email could easily mean losing your money to even an amateur attacker.

Address Allowlisting

A feature that some exchanges offer that may save the day in the event of account compromise is that of address allowlisting. This feature allows a user to configure a predefined set of external addresses that the exchange account is permitted to send to. When you store cryptocurrency in an exchange, you're not actually given the keys to that address. But many users will eventually send coins out of the exchange and into a mobile wallet or a hardware wallet, for example. Since the addresses of those wallets are known to you, you can set up your exchange account so that it can only create transactions that go to those addresses. This does present somewhat of a privacy risk as you are likely going to re-use those addresses for multiple transactions. However, you are already revealing your addresses to the exchange to transact in the first place, so there's not a large privacy risk using this feature.

If an attacker gains access to an exchange account, their ultimate goal is usually to send those coins out to their own wallets, so that they are now the sole owner of those coins. It usually does not do them much good to just sit inside your account and control it, giving you time to notice that something is wrong. They simply want your money – meaning they must send the coins to an address for which they control the private keys.

By using the address allowlisting feature, you can prevent an attacker from sending coins out to *their* addresses. Your account will be set up to only allow sends to *your* addresses. Most exchanges with an allowlist feature have a set period of time before a new address can be added to the list. So, for example, if you generate a new address from a hardware wallet you'd like to list, you must wait 48 hours until you can actually send coins out to that address. In the meantime, you'll just have to wait or send coins to an already-allowed destination.

This buys you precious time in the event your account is compromised. Let's imagine your Coinbase password is phished, and an attacker is able to gain access to your account. Coinbase notes this new login and sends you an email about it, but it's already too late. Within 5 minutes, the attacker creates a new blockchain transaction sending all of your bitcoin and ether to their own addresses, an irreversible theft. But imagine that you have allowlisting enabled instead. This time, the attacker tries to send coins out to their address but is denied by a prompt telling them they must add to the allowed address book first and wait 48 hours. Within an hour or so of the initial compromise you notice the email stating there's a new login that wasn't you. You immediately lock your account, change your password, and regain sole access with no money lost. This feature was the difference between an annoying afternoon of support calls and permanently losing all of your money.

Browser Hygiene

As with all software, it's important to keep our *web browser* up to date. Ensuring our browser has the latest software updates will prevent vulnerabilities from threatening our crypto assets. Web applications such as exchanges are complex and contain a lot of moving parts code wise, and therefore a myriad of opportunities for attacks. Allowing our browser software to become stale could allow attackers to exploit vulnerabilities and steal your authentication tokens, credentials, or even install malware on your system.

Browser *extensions* require the same amount of care. These bits of software are particularly powerful and allow more access to our system than a typical web application or web site you visit. These require installing software on your system and allow powerful interaction like autofilling passwords or storing sensitive data like crypto keys. Crypto wallet extensions such as

Metamask are commonly used. While convenient, these extensions can be exploited by attackers to drain your funds. Be careful interacting with websites that ask you to connect to these extensions, as malicious wallet drainers can empty you out in an instant. As well, extension software must also be kept up to date and free of vulnerabilities. A malicious extension could steal your keys, swap your copy/pasted addresses for an attacker's, or even install additional malware on your system that does one of those things.

Finally, take advantage of browsers or extensions that provide convenient security services. For example, extensions that enable HTTPS Everywhere. This feature ensures that all sites you visit upgrade to use TLS/HTTPS – meaning that all traffic between you and the website is encrypted, protecting your credentials and other sensitive information as they transit across the internet. As we discussed earlier, password managers are an important tool for security. Many managers have browser extensions such as 1Password or Bitwarden. These tools make it easy to generate, store, and autofill those long, strong passphrases right at the websites you visit. This convenient security software can enhance your hygiene by making it easier to follow good credential practices.

Part 3

Self-Custody Security

Part 3, Chapter 1

Self-Custody Security Basics

The beauty of cryptocurrency is self-sovereignty. The ability to truly hold your own money, rather than trusting a third party, reduces the sort of counterparty risk we encounter in the traditional banking system. If you hold the keys to your own Bitcoin, Ether, or other coins – you are the rightful owner, and can spend at any time without asking for permission. Many of us are used to a world where we can access our money at any time, with minimal restrictions on purchases and transfers. But this is not always the case – many in the world are at risk of having bank accounts seized, transactions stopped, and other restrictions placed on their financial freedom. Decentralized digital currencies have no such restrictions.

In some respects, cryptocurrency exchanges or custodial wallets mirror the relationship we have with traditional banks. In this model, we relegate control of the actual keys to the custodian. When we need to send coins from our account, they ensure that we have the right amount in their database, then sign the actual blockchain transaction with their keys. In this model, the end user doesn't have direct access to the private keys used for signing. Instead, we trade self-sovereignty for convenience. Since exchange accounts usually have a username, password, and 2FA like any other online account, this level of technology is more accessible for many users. Although trusting an exchange involves some level of risk, the overall security posture of a reputable exchange may be higher than what an end-user can attain. If you're unsure of how to hold your private keys altogether, it’s better to let cybersecurity and crypto experts handle that work for you. It's worthwhile to do some reading on any exchange you choose to use – get an idea of how long they have been in business, any major issues they have had, and how those issues were handled before using them for large amounts of money.

That said, the ultimate security and self-sovereignty in crypto comes from learning to manage your own private keys. In this model, you and you alone are responsible for the safety of your crypto. When done properly, self-custody of keys will yield the highest level of security for any given user. There’s no trust that must be given to a third party. Generally, an end user is a smaller target for theft than a major exchange. And ultimately, no authority can decide what you do with that money. There’s no way for someone to censor a transaction coming from a self-custody wallet. You have the power to send that money to anyone, anywhere in the world, at any time – just a transaction signature away.

This model does come with serious risks, however. Learning to secure keys against the countless threats and user errors out there does involve dedicated study and mindfulness. The next chapters will dive into the secure management of cryptocurrency private keys, for various wallets you are likely to encounter. First, we’ll discuss the types of self-custody wallets available, and look at their pros and cons. Next, we’ll dive into the security of hot wallets – the kind you’ll have on a PC or mobile phone. Finally, we’ll discuss cold wallets, which are generally the highest level of security. All of this will be discussed with a focus on common pitfalls, practical security tips, and an emphasis on why we want to follow these practices.

The Importance of Crypto Asset Private Key Management

This may seem obvious to some readers of this book already, but it is still worth saying: your private keys control *everything* in the cryptocurrency world. Throughout these chapters, we'll be using the terms private key and seed phrase interchangeably even though these are slightly different formats, because losing either to an attacker has the same result. Whoever has access to the keys has unfettered access to all of your assets. Losing your crypto keys is not the same thing as losing a password. If you lose a password, someone may temporarily access your account until you can lock it, call customer support, or take some other action to restore your account. If your seed phrase is compromised, however, the attacker can, and likely will, immediately transfer all coins and tokens to their own addresses. Crypto transactions are irreversible by design, and that means your money is gone – period.

The higher consequences of losing keys means we should treat them with special care, beyond what we might do with critical passwords. Avoiding theft is important, of course. We don't want any unauthorized users to gain access to the keys and therefore all of our money. But outside attackers aren't the only threat to the safety of our digital assets. Key *loss* is as important to protect against as key *theft*. There's no "forgot password" feature for self-custody crypto wallets. If you lose the key data, you lose access to the coins permanently.

As part of our plan for security, we will approach both the risks of key theft and key loss. Protecting keys from unauthorized access by ensuring proper storage will prevent attackers from taking the juicy reward sitting in our wallets. Protecting keys from loss will prevent our own mistakes or outside forces of nature from rendering our coins permanently inaccessible. Proper backups of the key data matter for both of these threats. Exactly how we store our keys makes all the difference in our overall security posture. How we back up our keys will vary depending on the type of wallet used to generate the keys in the first place, and what our overall threat model looks like.

Part 3, Chapter 2

Types of Self-Custody Wallets

In order to understand how to properly store our cryptocurrency keys, it is first helpful to understand the types of wallets available to us. The type of wallet will dictate the overall level of security, and how we should manage our backups to maintain that same amount of security.

At a core level, a wallet is a piece of software that generates and stores Bitcoin keys, generates addresses from those keys, and digitally signs transactions. At some point along the way, a fully functioning wallet must also be able to get data on address balances from the public blockchain in order to construct transactions for signing. This work can either be done by a full node, which validates and stores all transactions, or a light client that just gets data about the specific addresses for that wallet. Modern wallets generate a *seed phrase*, a single master key that can be used to derive unlimited individual key and public address pairs. Wallets can also generate single private key and address pairs at random without the use of a seed, but seed phrases are the modern standard.

At the very simplest level though, a "wallet" is just a single private key and address pair. One could generate a key, derive the address, and receive as much money as they like to that address without even having an internet connection. Of course, you would have to later "sweep" that key into a more fully-functioned wallet to spend those coins. But you don't have to have anything more than a key and address to have a very basic cryptocurrency wallet.

Given that a wallet can be anything from a single private key and address pair all the way to a fully-validating blockchain node, there's a lot of room for developers to provide different kinds of wallet software. Pretty much any platform that can run code can run Bitcoin wallet software of some level – from tiny microprocessors, to mobile phones, all the way up to powerful desktop computers. Just as many software developers try to "run Doom" (a popular video game) on just about every possible type of computer, many developers "run Bitcoin" across a wide variety of devices.

As we'll see later on, the simplest form of wallet doesn't even need a computer for storage – you can encode a seed phrase or single key data on paper or metal and store it for later use, eschewing digital storage for the simple physical form. That key data must be generated on a computing device and swept when you want to spend it, but the wallet can exist in purely physical form for as long as you desire simple, reliable storage. Most wallets offer key generation, storage, address management, and transaction signing.

Some terminology – a *hot* wallet is a wallet that runs on an internet-connected computing device. Most commonly, this is a desktop PC or a mobile phone. These wallets generate and store the keys on an internet-connected machine, which as we will see offers less security than the other type of wallet. A *cold* wallet is a wallet where the keys are stored (and often generated) on an *offline* device. These are usually purpose-built, retail devices designed for crypto like Trezor, Ledger, KeepKey, and others.

Hot Wallets

Desktop or PC Wallets

Desktop and PC wallets, you guessed it, run on full-fledged PCs like desktop or laptop computers. These wallets can be installed on common operating systems like Windows, Mac OSX, and Linux. Due to the ease of development and available computing power, storage, and bandwidth, these can be some of the most feature-complete wallets available.

In most cases, fully validating nodes must run in a desktop setting. Full nodes download, validate, and re-broadcast the entire blockchain for a given cryptocurrency. This function is particularly important for open blockchains such as Bitcoin and Ethereum, which need lots of full nodes to decentralize the validation of transactions. This offers security and privacy advantages as there's no need to ask or trust a third party to validate your transactions, or fetch data in order to construct them. Full nodes help support the network by providing additional copies of the blockchain others can use and enforcing the rules by validating transactions. Because a full node must store a copy of the entire blockchain, receive and rebroadcast transactions, and validate a large number of cryptographic operations, the required resources go beyond what smaller devices can reasonably achieve. A desktop PC has the requisite storage, bandwidth, and computing power to run these full nodes.

That's not to say all desktop wallets are full nodes. In fact, many desktop wallets are light clients: wallets that rely on 3rd parties such as full nodes or blockchain explorers to fetch selected transaction data. These wallets still allow the user to have full control over their own private keys and thus are non-custodial, but they do ask full nodes for transaction data. In either case, desktop wallets offer a simple, familiar way to interact with cryptocurrency networks and retain full control over user private keys.

A major advantage of desktop wallets is the ability to run a full node. For those that wish to exercise the full power of cryptocurrency and validate a blockchain, a desktop wallet is necessary. Another advantage of this wallet is familiarity and ease-of-use for those used to regular old computer software. Most find the workflow of installing and using software on a PC familiar, so backups, transactions, and troubleshooting will feel easier than other types of wallets.

A major disadvantage of these wallets is overall security. Although running a full node, for example, contributes to the overall security of the network, desktop wallets have several disadvantages for end-user private key security. This is largely due to a higher *attack surface* than other types of wallets. This means there are more avenues for someone to potentially compromise your keys or steal from you in other ways using desktop wallets.

First, malware can exist on the PC and attempt to steal keys or swap addresses out for those of an attacker. Secondly, PC software installation is generally friction-free. There's no real verification of the software required to install it, so you could be installing *malicious* wallet software without knowing it. There have been several instances of malicious actors tricking users into installing fake wallet software and stealing cryptocurrency. With hardware wallets and mobile wallets, this threat is less likely although not impossible.

Mobile Wallets

Mobile wallets are installed on smartphone devices such as Android or iOS. Of course, we are talking about non-custodial mobile wallets which aren't the same as an exchange app. These wallets allow users to fully control their own keys and easily sign transactions from their mobile device. These wallets range in functionality from fairly simple to complex, depending on the currencies and protocol features supported. In particular, these wallets are often designed with convenience in mind.

Given that smartphones are portable and usually carried around with us, these wallets generally offer the greatest convenience for everyday spending. With your camera, you can scan a QR code to get a payment address instead of typing or copy-pasting it. Wallets are usually light clients that require a connection to other nodes or a server for payment info, so the software has a small footprint on your device. Many wallets are designed to support multiple currencies, tokens, and protocol features for payments and smart contracts.

You might think that this convenience comes at the price of security, but mobile wallets are actually a better choice for security than desktop due to the lower attack surface. Mobile operating systems, by design, are more locked-down than a typical PC OS. Every application must ask permission to access sensitive system resources such as the camera, storage, or location. The programming interface and libraries are standardized and well maintained. And the vast majority of users download apps from a central app store. These stores, Google Play and the Apple App Store, vet apps in advance for standard requirements and scan for malware. Although it is possible to download apps from a 3rd party on Android, most users will go through the app store.

All of these security features mean there's less chance for malware to infect your device and less chance for a malicious wallet to get into the app store. Keep in mind that it's not impossible for this to happen, and some malicious apps have stolen user funds. One such example scans the user's photos for seed phrases using optical character recognition and pattern-matching code. It's just less likely than on a PC where it's standard practice to install software from all over the internet with little vetting. The permissions ecosystem on mobile also makes it less likely that malware could scan your clipboard for addresses, scan your filesystem for keys, or execute other attacks.

Cold Wallets

Hardware Wallets

Cold wallets are the pinnacle of cryptocurrency security for most users. The term cold wallet most often refers to hardware wallets, which are specialized devices designed for generating, storing, and using cryptocurrency keys. Devices such as Trezor, Ledger, and KeepKey are commercially available devices built with commonly available microprocessors, and usually with open-source software – called firmware in this context.

Hardware wallets such as these commercial examples are fully featured and specially designed for the safe storage of crypto keys. These wallets generate your keys completely offline and store them encrypted in such a way that they cannot be extracted from the device. By connecting your wallet to a PC, you can sign and broadcast transactions without the keys ever leaving the device. You can also connect a hardware wallet to a PC running a full node rather than relying on other servers for transaction data, while keeping your keys on the device.

A cold wallet doesn't have to be this complicated, even. A keypair generated on an offline PC or simple microcontroller can be printed, written down, or etched in metal. The address associated with the key or seed can be used to receive funds as long as you like, while keeping the key safe offline. You would later have to import that key into a hot wallet for spending, however, thereby reducing your security. Full-featured hardware wallets have the advantage here because they can also sign transactions while keeping the keys offline.

Hardware or other cold wallets offer the best security for users. This approach has the lowest attack surface of all wallet options, because compromising the keys would generally require *physical* access to the user's seed phrase or private key backups. Since the keys are generated and stored on a non-networked, specialized device, there's no chance for malicious software to extract keys and send them off to the attacker. There's a small chance of supply-chain related attacks tainting the device firmware, or a user being tricked into installing a malicious firmware update. However, this is still less likely to occur than some other malware or exploit finding its way onto a general-purpose phone or PC.

Less software and no networking mean these devices have fewer chances to be tainted by malicious code, snooping, or even user interaction. And beyond the device, the storage of cold wallet key backups offers distinct advantages. Cold wallet key data such as seed phrases or encoded private keys must always be stored in offline and or non-electronic form. Most often, this data is written on paper or stamped into metal. By only storing keys offline, you avoid the possibility that malware can extract keys, send them to an attacker, or allow for attempted decryption. Offline keys require physical access to steal rather than network access, which is a much less likely threat/risk for the average user.

Part 3, Chapter 3

Hot Wallet Security – Key Backups

The Art of Backups

As we've discussed, the core of cryptocurrency ownership is private keys. Ultimately, to spend cryptocurrency, you must have access to those keys used for digital signatures of transactions. Access to keys means you can spend. No access to keys means you cannot. Crypto educator Andreas M. Antonopoulos coined the term "Not Your Keys, Not Your Coins" – an apt phrase for this world of self-sovereign money.

But digital devices are certainly fallible, as are their users. Hard drives fail. Solid state memory chips go bad. People drop their phones in the toilet. Natural disasters such as fire or flood render electronic data wholly unrecoverable. There's a lot of ways the primary storage device for your wallet can fail. What happens if your electronic wallet is destroyed? Again, you *must* have access to your keys to spend your coins. There is no forgot password feature for self-custody wallets, and no bank to contact for help.

Thus, maintaining solid backups is critical for your overall security posture as a self-custody crypto user. A *backup* is simply a redundant copy of the key data, stored somewhere other than the primary storage device. There's lots of reasonable ways to back up digital data in general, but greater care is required when discussing cryptographic keys.

In general, backups of data should follow the *3-2-1 rule*. This rule starts with the idea that you have three total copies of the data, including the primary. That means your primary data storage and two separate backups. This rule also recommends that you use two different forms of storage media for your data. For example, two copies might be stored on a traditional hard disk drive (HDD) and the other stored on a solid-state drive (SSD). The third part of this rule recommends that one copy of the data resides offsite, meaning some physical location other than the primary storage place. For many folks, using cloud storage services will cover this requirement.

When we're talking about crypto keys though, it's not as simple as just replicating the data. How the backups are secured and accessed makes a big difference in overall security. It's not enough for our data to be backed up, it must also have strict access control and data confidentiality in order to be safe against theft. In practical terms, that means your data should be only accessible by you (or your heirs in the event of your passing), and your data should be encrypted.

Seed Phrase Backups: Physical

We know that our wallet, most likely, will give us a *seed phrase* that encodes all the information needed to generate an infinite number of private keys and addresses for our wallet. Seed phrases offer the most convenient way to back up key data compared to individual keys or sets of keys. Backing up a seed phrase can start with one of the most secure ways to store these bits, without involving a computer at all – paper!

A great place to start backing up your seed phrase is simply to write it down and store it somewhere safe. Write your seed using a pen or permanent marker on durable paper. Consider laminating that paper if you have the tools to do so. Store that copy somewhere secure from fire, flood, and unauthorized access. If you have a safe available, that can be a great place to store your seed. These are often resistant to fire and water, and a good safe is resistant to break in.

There can be some problems with this though. Of course, as a medium, paper isn't the most durable. It is vulnerable to fire and flood, fading, or contamination rendering the key data unreadable. Another alternative that has emerged is to put the seed in metal, a much more durable medium. Several commercial solutions exist for etching or stamping seeds into metal. You could even use stamps and metal from the hardware store to do so. This option makes your seed far more resistant to fire, and flooding may or may not be a problem depending on the metal used. You want a material that has a high melting point and resists corrosion easily. Again, storing this in a safe adds an additional layer of protection against the elements.

A nice part of this approach is that it also may make wallet access easier for your heirs should something happen to you, or if you make a mistake with your primary wallet and need to recover. Backups should generally be easy to access and easy to recover from. Imagine you need to recover your wallet after upgrading to a new phone. With a paper or metal seed, you would first reinstall the software on the new phone and import the seed by reading off of the physical medium and typing it into the wallet. This would generally take a minute or so, with little friction.

However, with no encryption and the seed sitting in your house on a piece of paper, there is always the risk of physical theft. A raw seed phrase can easily be imported into pretty much any wallet that supports the BIP39 and BIP44 standards. So, if someone theoretically breaks into your house and finds your raw seed, you could lose your money.

Realistically, you should think about what your threat model is. Unless you're a high-profile individual or someone that constantly talks about cryptocurrency wealth online, you're not that likely to have someone target you, break into your house, steal your safe, take the time to crack it open, and steal all your coins. If you *do* have that threat model, that's a bit beyond the scope of this book and I would recommend getting some consulting from a security professional.

For most folks, preventing basic smash-and-grab theft or simple mistakes is more of an issue. You probably don't need your seed phrase under the same strict security controls of banks and data centers, but you don't want it just lying around either. Take some time to think about a safe, but accessible place for data storage. Perhaps you have a special drawer that you use only for important documents, or a simple fire box, or a wall safe. All are reasonable places to store crypto keys that balance security with convenience.

Seed Phrase and Key Backups: Digital

For hot wallets, there is also the possibility of digital seed phrase or key backups. Why can we use digital backups for hot wallets but not cold wallets? Essentially, it's about the overall "level" of security. With a hot wallet, the keys are generated and stored (in encrypted form) on a general purpose, networked device. A PC wallet stores keys on a PC, a mobile wallet on a mobile phone. The keys are stored encrypted, so that nobody without the wallet passphrase or PIN can access the keys directly. If you store a backup of the keys on a digital device also in encrypted form, you haven't done much to change the overall level of security of the keys. Whereas, storing a cold wallet seed on a networked device would break the security model of that type of wallet entirely, as the entire point is to avoid the internet when generating and storing keys.

If you wish to store an encrypted backup of your hot wallet keys, it's important to do so in a way that conforms to security best practices, as this does add an additional point of failure. First, you should use well-vetted software designed for storing keys or other secrets using strong encryption. Software like a password manager can be a good fit for this purpose. A password manager is purpose-built for storing secrets, while also designed for ease of use. If you have some technical know-how, you could also opt for some other strong encryption method like a VeraCrypt container, an AES-encrypted file via OpenSSL, or use of a GPG key. Those options require more technical savvy than using something like 1Password, KeePass, or another secrets manager.

It's important the software you use has strong encryption such as AES. Simple password-protection is not enough and can be bypassed by malicious actors. The password must be used as a key for actual encryption. When data is properly encrypted, someone with the ciphertext (meaning the encrypted form of the data), cannot access it in any way without first decrypting it using the key. They would need to know your password (or potentially crack that password) to get the seed phrase inside.

The most important thing to NOT do when it comes to seed phrases is to store them electronically in any plaintext (meaning unencrypted) form. This includes text documents, Word documents, Google Docs, pictures, or screenshots. There are several reasons for this. First, it's possible for you to leak your key data by accident in the form of a mis-shared picture or document. Second, and more of a threat in this context, is that an attacker can steal your keys through malware. Seed-scanning malware that finds its way onto your system can look for the pattern of a seed phrase and wipe your wallet clean. Or someone who compromises your cloud storage through phishing would have direct access to your money. Certainly, having a bad actor reading your files is bad – but recoverable. Someone stealing your crypto via a seed phrase is permanent.

Some wallets, although rare these days, don't use seed phrases and instead store sets of individual keys. The original "wallet.dat" Bitcoin Core wallets are a good example of this. These wallets periodically generate addresses and store them encrypted in the wallet file. This was sometimes problematic for high-transaction-volume users, because the wallet would have to generate additional addresses to avoid reuse when the existing set was used up. This means that you'd have to periodically update your wallet file backups to ensure all keys were stored in that backup. Seed phrases by contrast can be used to generate infinite addresses in a deterministic way, avoiding this problem.

Backing up encrypted wallet files securely is fairly straightforward. You must choose a long, strong encryption passphrase for your wallet so that it's secured against password cracking attacks. Provided you do that, you can back it up the same way you'd do any other import data like documents, pictures, code, or videos. You can follow the 3-2-1 rule and replicate a few copies of your encrypted wallet, using different media, and ensuring at least one backup is off site. Unlike a raw seed phrase, this wallet is already encrypted so no additional layers of encryption are required.

Part 3, Chapter 4

Hot Wallet Security – Software Hygiene

Safe Software Installation

Safe and secure backups ensure your cryptocurrency keys remain in your hands, and not those of an attacker. But we must also ensure the software that generates those keys in the first place is legitimate and secure. Malicious crypto software remains a devious avenue for attackers to steal your coins. In order to install safe software, there's several practices we can follow.

For mobile wallets, one of the simplest ways we can ensure safe installation is to only download from the official app store for our device. For Android, this is the Google Play store. For Apple, this is the App Store. This is not a guarantee of safe software, and malicious apps can sometimes make it into these stores. However, the vetting process that app developers must follow generally works well and prevents a good chunk of malicious code from getting onto end-user devices. This process will likely catch malware that might do something like swap addresses or scan your phone for keys. It may or may not be good enough to catch issues like poor-entropy key generation, but it's a start.

Another practice that can be helpful here is to look at the account and number of installations for a particular app. Although we all wish to give new developers a chance to grow, it's generally safer to choose popular and therefore well-tested crypto applications. If you wish to install something like Coinbase Wallet or Coinomi, it's simple to check that the app link and developer name match the link on the main website for that company. Coinomi, for example, has a link on their website to download the Android app. If you search "Coinomi" in Google Play, ensure the information matches. Checking that the app has a substantial number of downloads and reviews, while imperfect, can also lend some credibility. We know that Coinbase is a popular exchange, so a fake "Coinbase" app with a few thousand downloads would be a bit suspicious.

For Desktop software, the vetting process is a bit more complicated. Anyone can write and distribute software for a PC, and unless you're going through something like the Microsoft store for every application, there's little vetting. Anyone can host a software download on their site that you can install without any significant warnings or barriers. That said, there are also best practices we can follow to ensure the validity of our finance-critical software.

First, try to navigate directly to the known main website of a company or open-source project for the software we wish to use. Relying directly on Google, Bing, DuckDuckGo searches can be misleading, as ad spaces have been used to trick users into installing malicious software. Be wary of URLs that look *similar* to the target, such as E1ectrum.org (with a one in place of the l) instead of Electrum.org.

More importantly, it's a great practice to learn how to verify software files' hashes and signatures when downloading. Wallets like Electrum, as an example, provide a *hash* and a *signature* alongside their software binaries. Hashes and signatures are used to verify both the *integrity* and *authenticity* of the software, respectively.

Integrity means verifying that a message (in this case, our software) has not been tampered with in transit. So, for example, ensuring that the software downloaded correctly from a website or was passed along from a repository without tampering.

Hash functions are commonly used for this purpose. A website or repository that shares software downloads will often include the hash of that binary alongside the software itself. To verify the integrity of a software download, the user runs a hashing algorithm on the file contents. Often, SHA-256 is used as it is a common, secure algorithm. The user verifies that the SHA-256 hash of the downloaded software matches exactly with the one provided from the website.

Cryptographic hashes are excellent for this purpose as even one bit of difference between files results in radically different values, meaning it's easy to visually and computationally verify the integrity of the software. The hash is also sometimes called the *fingerprint.*

Using hash functions for integrity sounds like enough, right? Verifying the hash/fingerprint means the software hasn't been tampered with from the website, so that must mean it is the legitimate bits we want. Well, not quite. This method does, indeed, verify that the software hasn't been tampered with from website to user. But what if the website itself is compromised? Maybe an attacker gained access to a web server and replaced both the software and the hash. How can we be sure our software came from the intended author? This is *authentication* – verifying that software came from the expected sender.

Digital signatures are used for this purpose. Digital signatures use similar asymmetric cryptography to that used for Bitcoin keys and addresses. The software publisher uses their private key to sign the software. Anyone with a copy of the public key can verify the signature, but nobody can create a signed software package without the secret private key. This provides our authentication scheme – anyone can easily verify that a signed package only came from the person with the right private key.

By learning to verify hashes and signatures, we can help ensure the software we're downloading for our cryptocurrency wallets is legitimate. Although this process takes some time and a bit of technical learning, it's a critical step for the security of our assets. Taking the time to learn this process can save us from the greater pain of having coins stolen by a malicious application.

Software and Device Maintenance

Once we have legitimate, safe wallet software installed, we must maintain it. Usually, this process is hands off and straightforward, with the application auto-updating or prompting the user to manually install periodic updates. Any vulnerabilities should be promptly patched to avoid malicious actors exploiting them. Patching is a software industry term for applying updated code that fixes a bug or vulnerability.

Our overall device hygiene must be maintained as well. Whether you are using Windows, Mac OSX, or Linux, make sure you have a reasonable anti-malware program installed and run it regularly. Keep up with operating system software updates so that attackers can't exploit serious vulnerabilities to run malicious code on your machine. If you're using Android or iOS, don't ignore your phone's prompts to install operating system updates.

Take care with what non-crypto-related software you install. Game cheats, pirated software, and other common avenues for malware can trick you into installing address-swapping or seed-scanning malware without you even knowing that your crypto is being targeted. If you're installing cryptocurrency wallets on your daily-driver computer, take extra care to audit what other software you have on the computer and run those malware scans.

Part 3, Chapter 5

Cold Wallet Security – Key Backups

Cold vs. Hot Wallet Backups

In a previous chapter, we discussed the critical nature of key backups, and in particular, ways in which you can safely back up the keys for your hot wallets. Ensuring safe backups means you can retain access to your crypto assets in the event the device with the main wallet is destroyed, lost, stolen, or otherwise loses the cryptographic key data. We won't rehash all the reasons backups are important here. However, there are some key differences in how to safely back up *cold wallet* keys in contrast with *hot wallet* keys.

Cold wallets, by definition, are wallets that generate and store the cryptographic keys for your assets *offline*. This means using a device that is not connected to the internet. Common commercial solutions you are likely to encounter include Trezor, Ledger, KeepKey, ColdCard, and others. These devices are microcontroller based, with special firmware designed solely for generating keys, storing them, and digitally signing your transactions. By design, you connect these devices to a networked computer via USB, but the keys never leave the device. So, you can construct a transaction using your PC and broadcast it to the network, something your hardware wallet device cannot do by itself. But the *signing* of that transaction occurs only on the hardware device, such that the keys are never transmitted or revealed in any way to the PC, and by extension, the threats that PC might be hiding.

This offline property of hardware or cold wallets is central to the security model. It's only a cold wallet if the keys are always offline. If the keys for a particular cold wallet do end up on a networked device, that's now a hot wallet. This understanding of the cold storage security model informs what types of backups we can safely choose for the key data. In keeping with the definition of a cold wallet, our backups must also be offline in nature.

The most effective and safe way to store hardware wallet seed phrases is to etch, stamp, or otherwise confer them into a durable storage medium such as metal. Several varying commercial products allow you to do this. Remember, we only have to store 12-24 English words to keep our entire BIP39-compatible wallet backed up. Any way that we can store that data into a long-lasting medium like metal will do. Paper is also a perfectly fine medium for this, but is more susceptible to environmental contamination such as water or fire. The most important thing is to ensure all the words are readable, in the correct order, and stored somewhere safe.

First, you must ensure that the 12 to 24 words are legible, and in the correct order. The words are ultimately encoding 128 to 256 bits of binary information, and the order does matter. The final word contains a cryptographic *checksum*, which the computer uses to indicate if something is wrong with the previous words. Storing words out of order or accidentally losing the order could result in a significant computational effort to find the correct order of words by guessing, something that may be entirely impossible or at least infeasible depending on how many words are out of order. Take care to note the correct order so that your future self can easily determine it. Placing a number in front of each word is a simple solution that makes this clear.

Legibility is also, while somewhat obvious, something to take care with. It's easy for us humans to write something down in poor handwriting and still understand what was written while the contents are in the front of our minds. But imagine yourself trying to interpret your wild scrawl ten years in the future, hoping desperately to recover tens of thousands of dollars' worth of digital assets stored in words you can't seem to read. Taking your time to transfer the words in a timelessly readable way ensures that you can actually restore from backup. Take the time to carefully read the words back to yourself, pretending that you don't remember what you just wrote down. A backup should be tested, after all.

As with hot wallets, there is the possibility that you can have a single-key cold wallet. The old-school *paper wallet* strategy, while ill-advised at the time of this writing, can certainly be used. The same rules apply – ensure that all the characters of the WIF (Wallet Import Format), or hexadecimal encoded data are legible and distinguishable from one another. This is particularly important for the random nature of single-key data. Take extra care to ensure that your alphabetic characters are clearly upper or lowercase, for example. Case matters with WIF keys, whereas seed phrases are case-insensitive. The base58 system used for Bitcoin and Litecoin's WIF format includes characters such as U and V that are hard to tell apart between upper and lower case. Adding a clear underscore for uppercase, for example, can be helpful. Base58 omits certain characters such as uppercase O and 0 to make this process a bit easier, but mistakes can still be made.

Next we must consider the storage of our backups, and the number of copies. Recall from the hot wallet backup section the 3-2-1 rule. We want to have three total copies of the data, stored in two different storage media, with at least one offsite copy. Three total copies is still a great rule for hardware wallet data. The “two” part is a bit less relevant here, as paper and metal are timeless media and don’t suffer from the same problems of bit rot and obsolescence as digital data. It’s perfectly fine to have all of your hardware wallet seed phrases written on paper, or all etched into metal, provided those copies are all cleanly stored.

The “one offsite” rule is a bit trickier when it comes to hardware wallet seeds. This rule is seriously important when it comes to recoverability and resistance to natural disasters. Imagine a fire or flood corrupting your only backups of your seed on paper or metal, rendering them completely destroyed or unreadable. This scenario must be protected against, and is one of the reasons metal is preferable to paper in many cases. A solid, stainless type of metal can resist fire and flood much more easily than even laminated paper. However, what about the issue of theft?

Our offsite backup will likely protect against a serious natural disaster, but it also must resist outright theft of the data. With 12-24 words simply written down, it’s not that unlikely that someone who knows what those words mean could walk away with the backup and steal your coins. Somewhat ironically, the traditional banking system can come to the aid of cryptocurrency users here. Renting a cheap safe-deposit box to store a copy of your seed gives you a backup that’s highly resistant to both theft, and fire and flood in most cases. This storage may be more problematic when considering the possibility of government seizure of crypto assets. If this is part of your threat model (depending on your location in the world), consider another option such as storage with a trusted family member or friend. Ensure your trusted partner stores the seed in a secure location such as a safe.

On some level, all of these backup methods, both primary and secondary, rely heavily on the assumption that your physical security is assured. An inexpensive safe in your residential home, a safe-deposit box from a trusted banking institution, or a safe in the home of a trusted friend or family member may not be available to you. If you live in a volatile situation physically, you should consider who might try to steal your seed or how it may be lost when moving from place to place. You should always keep the backup whole and intact, but you can get somewhat creative with storage provided that you can *always* remember where your backup is stored and how to access it in case of an emergency or other situation where key data must be retrieved. Recommendations on security for those (such as crypto celebrities) who might be directly targeted for theft are beyond the scope of this book. Consider consulting a security professional for a tailored safety and security plan if physical attack is a part of your threat profile.

Your overall strategy should balance these several factors. First, ensure you have several working copies of your seed or other key data. That means copies that you've carefully created, ensuring ordering and legibility of the key data. Next, protect the seed against natural forces that might corrupt the data. Consider fire, flood, accidental disposal, and other things that might render your key data missing or unreadable. Third, consider protection against theft. Secure your seed in a location that would be difficult for an intruder to access, such as a safe or a bank safe-deposit box.

All of these measures will ensure that your keys remain accessible and usable if and when they are needed to restore access to a cold wallet. Your hardware device serves as the primary key storage and signing mechanism, but digital copies must always be backed up by physical seed phrases. In the odd case of a paper wallet or other single-key data, you should still make backups in case the primary paper wallet is rendered unreadable. Take care that you have disaster and theft resistant backups so you never lose access to your coins in a worst-case scenario. Remember: with a non-custodial wallet, there is no forgot password feature. You are solely responsible for the safety of your keys.

Part 3, Chapter 6

Cold Wallet Security – Additional Strategies

Layering Protection with Passphrases

You may have noticed a glaring issue with the previous chapters on both hot and cold wallet backups. In many cases, the recommendation is to store a paper or metal copy of the standard seed words somewhere safe. These seed words grant access to all the coins in the cryptocurrency wallet, and therefore serve as a useful backup in case the primary device such as a hardware wallet malfunctions. Of course, we want to store those words in a safe place where they are unlikely to be stolen. But what happens if they are?

We have a reasonable concern about what happens if someone does get unauthorized physical access to your seed words, especially since a cold wallet likely contains the highest value of coins in your personal crypto ecosystem. Some sort of hack compromising your spending-money hot-wallet seed would result in a loss of funds that would be difficult, but hopefully manageable. But someone stealing the seed to your cold wallet, perhaps containing your crypto life-savings, could be catastrophic.

This book assumes that you're an average everyday user that doesn't have targeted physical theft as part of your threat model, but theft is still possible. Perhaps the cleaning person at your house is crypto aware, and steals your seed. Perhaps a petty criminal breaks into your house, walks away with your document safe, and knows what to do with a set of seed words. What happens then?

Thankfully, there is a way to *layer* the security of your seed words, and buy yourself time in the event such a theft occurs. There's a tool at our disposal called a *BIP39 Passphrase*. This is a standard part of the protocol for seed words that allows you to derive your wallet from additional data besides the randomly generated 12-24 words. This is sometimes called a 13th word (or 25th word), but I think this terminology is a bit of a misnomer. The additional "word" can be any passphrase the user chooses, and does not have to be a single additional word from the BIP39 dictionary. In fact, a single word from that dictionary would, in most cases, insufficiently resist a determined attacker.

Our passphrase should follow the same practices that we use for generating an exchange or custodial wallet passphrase. A random secret that's long and high entropy will greatly enhance the security of the overall wallet, and can save us from immediate compromise in the event the base key data is stolen. In most cases, we'll want a passphrase that is high entropy but also easy to type, store, or even memorize. A *diceware* passphrase generated by a computer or even real dice rolls is useful here. This technique takes entropy from a random source and selects English words from a predetermined dictionary. This allows us to generate passphrases that are memorable and easy to type, and higher in entropy (randomness) than a user-generated phrase.

Now, when we wish to interact with our hardware wallet, we'll enter this passphrase on top of the base key data that's stored in the device. This protects the safety of our crypto keys and addresses, even in the event the device is stolen or our raw seed phrase is compromised. The passphrase serves as an additional layer above our seed phrase backup, or above the encryption PIN on the hardware device.

This type of additional layer is also possible with single keypairs. BIP38 encryption (not to be confused with the BIP39 passphrase) allows the user to encrypt a single key using the specified passphrase, and copy the encrypted key in a special format for storage. This is particularly useful for single-keypair paper or metal wallets. Although these formats are less common and less robust than BIP39 seed phrases, it's still valuable to understand their security.

A BIP38 passphrase acts differently than a BIP39 passphrase. BIP38 encryption actually uses the passphrase to *encrypt* the key, and gives the user that ciphertext in a specially encoded format for storage. By contrast, BIP39 passphrases are used in *addition* to the plaintext seed words. The user needs the seed words and the passphrase to derive their keys and addresses. With encrypted single keys, you import the encoded key into a wallet while presenting the passphrase for decryption.

Now, we must think about how to safely store this additional data. This passphrase is a second factor for the wallet, much like an auth-app is a second factor for a passphrase. Given this, it's important that the passphrase is stored separately from the seed phrase or private key. Storing the passphrase right next to the key data would negate the value of having it, as an attacker could immediately steal it if they gain access to the location where both items are stored. This is a reasonable risk to take with something like an account passphrase plus 2FA recovery codes for a typical account, stored in a password manager. But for a hardware wallet, holding a significant amount of funds, we want to take every step to protect these factors independently.

An obvious step to take is to simply store the passphrase in physical form, in a different location than the seed phrase or key data. Follow the same rules as used for your primary key data – make sure the location is secure from theft, and the passphrase is resistant to fire and flood. Ensure that there are also secure backups, in a different location than the primary in case it is destroyed or lost. You must have access to both the key data and the passphrase to access your coins, so these backups are just as important.

One slight difference, however, is that it's also reasonable to store a copy of just the passphrase in encrypted digital form. Using a secure tool such as a password manager for the passphrase is reasonable, unlike the key data, because *just* the passphrase cannot be used to derive any keys and therefore sign transactions. The goal is for our cold wallet to have the base key data offline, away from networked devices always. But the passphrase itself could be stored with less overall risk to the system and without necessarily breaking the security model of a cold wallet. Whether you choose to store an encrypted backup or stay with the physical airgap is up to you.

I highly recommend the use of a passphrase for your hardware wallet if you're able to do so. This additional layer can save you from compromise in the event your key data is somehow stolen, however unlikely. It can also buy you time in the event you are accidentally victimized by a *phishing scam* and give your seed phrase to an attacker. Anyone trying to steal your keys would also have to guess the passphrase, giving you valuable time to realize your mistake and transfer coins to a new wallet before it's too late.

A final potentially useful strategy is the use of a *decoy wallet*. The BIP39 standard allows you to generate unlimited wallets using different passphrases. You may wish to put a smaller amount of money in a decoy wallet with an easier-to-guess passphrase, so an attacker trying possible phrases is likely to encounter the decoy funds first and stop their search. You can keep the more significant amount of money in a wallet with a much stronger passphrase. This strategy is particularly useful for a possible scenario where you are forced to give a wallet seed and passphrase under duress. If you're ever physically accosted for your crypto coins, you can give the attacker the decoy wallet information to keep yourself safe, while protecting the bulk of your assets.

A Note on Things You Shouldn't Do

Now we've discussed the deep importance of secure, offline seed phrase backups for cold wallets. As well, some additional security layers in the form of passphrases. Now is the time that many of us tech-savvy, paranoid, security-focused folks try to get...creative.

And creativity is not necessarily a great trait to have when it comes to security practices.

When I say creative, I mean trying to do non-standard things with your seed. Many individuals think it will add an extra layer of security to do things like seed-splitting – putting different sets of your seed words in different physical locations. Some users try to hide their seeds using steganography – hiding the seed in digital data like images, or spread throughout the pages in a book. You might even think about enciphering your words using some simple protocol like a Caesar cipher before writing them down.

All of these ideas actually introduce a greater danger than theft: key *loss*. The simple fact is that you're more likely to make a mistake and lose access to your seed than you are to have your seed stolen. You *think* you can remember your cool new protocol, but it's entirely possible that in five years when you need to access your seed (something you don't do often), you have no idea how to unscramble the words you've encoded in some odd format. Or you can't find one of three places in your home where you've split the seed. And of course, using these non-standard protocols greatly increases the chance that your heirs cannot access your crypto assets in the event something happens to you.

Follow standard protocols. The BIP39 standard is extremely well thought out in its details, like the fact you only need the first four characters of a word to know the whole word in case the seed is slightly damaged. The BIP39 passphrase allows you to import a seed and passphrase into almost any other cold or hot wallet. Standard encoding for single keys like WIF and BIP38 passphrases offers the same flexibility. Use these well thought out standards and follow best practices for storing your key backups, and avoid shooting yourself in the foot with “creative” tactics.

Bitcoin-Only Firmware

A software management strategy that may be helpful for users of single cryptocurrencies is single-crypto firmware. For example, Bitcoin-only software or Ethereum-only software for your device. As far as I am aware, this mostly applies to Bitcoin (BTC) as it is the most popular currency available and has a large community of people that only use Bitcoin and nothing else.

By installing Bitcoin-only firmware on your device, you’re simply reducing the amount of code that runs on it. And therefore, you reduce the risk of some bug or vulnerability being present in the software you’re running. Hardware wallet software is carefully vetted and crafted to be cryptographically secure, but all software is vulnerable to mistakes. Computers tend to execute code perfectly and predictably, but humans don’t always write it that way. Blame us software engineers.

If you know for a fact you’re only going to use Bitcoin on your device, installing Bitcoin-only firmware is a solid *attack surface* reduction strategy. Provided you’re able to securely install the software by downloading from a legitimate source, and verifying hashes and signatures, your overall risk profile may be slightly reduced. Why run software for 100 different cryptocurrencies if you are only using one? That’s a lot of opportunities for a vulnerability to sneak in.

Part 4

The Threat Landscape

Part 4, Chapter 1

The Threat Landscape

The most critical part to understanding the security of your digital assets is understanding what threatens those assets. Everything that we've discussed up to this point covers the mechanics of cryptocurrency security – the practical application of security techniques. But truly safeguarding your crypto wealth requires understanding why those practices exist in the first place.

Every security technique discussed in the previous chapters exists because of a particular risk that users currently face in the crypto landscape, or threats that real users have faced in the past. Regulations are written in blood, as they say. But in the cryptocurrency space, regulations are few. The reality, as we have discussed, is that *you* are solely responsible for your assets in most cases. Instead, we can say that security recommendations in crypto are written on the backs of someone out there that lost some or all of their money.

Crypto threats are multifaceted, and continuously evolving. These chapters are simply a snapshot of the threat landscape as of right now. Most of these threats and techniques for mitigating them will be relatively timeless, modifiable as both threat actors and cryptocurrency users evolve. Some may be out of date in a few years, and some threats we can't even imagine yet will plague the future. Such is the nature of fast-moving technology, especially when serious money is involved.

Luckily, we don’t have to have simple if-then statements for every possible threat that exists, used to exist, or will exist. Understanding the *patterns* that threat actors use and how to spot those patterns will allow us to mitigate those threats as they continue to change over time.

There are several broad patterns that users must understand when protecting against the loss of digital assets. First, we’ll look at phishing attacks – methods of tricking a user into giving up sensitive information such as seed phrases, private keys, passwords, or money outright. Next, malware and other technical threats to wallets, software, or transactions. And finally, we will consider self-induced loss through user error.

Part 4, Chapter 2

Phishing Tactics

Phishing is when attackers try to trick a user into giving up sensitive information – seed phrases and private keys, passwords, or even money. Anything that has value, an attacker may trick you into giving them. Phishing relies on attacking humans, rather than systems, as humans are often easier to crack than technology. We all have in-built tendencies that hackers can leverage – we become inattentive, we get greedy, and we act in a hurry.

One thing that phishers love is urgency. Many of us are busy, balancing our work, hobbies, and families. When something urgent comes up, we often want it done so we can get back to whatever important things we were doing before this chore presented itself. But urgency is a big disadvantage for security. Phishing scams that target your seed phrase might threaten to "deactivate" your wallet within 24 hours if you don't comply, so you quickly give up what they want to get back to your other tasks.

Another tactic phishing attacks commonly use is somewhat similar to that of urgency – threats. Phishers use the threat of some negative outcome to trick you into panicking and giving up what they want. Threats often come with urgency, because if you're scared and in a hurry, you're less likely to take the time to think about whether that threat is legitimate. Scams that pretend to be from a wallet might threaten to seize your assets if you don't comply.

If the threats and urgency don’t get you, a juicy reward just might. Who doesn’t love free money? Cryptocurrency airdrop and giveaway scams are a profitable tactic for phishers to part users from their valuable coins, because they tempt users with the promise of financial gain.

Part 4, Chapter 3

Fake Wallet or Exchange Tech Support Phishing

Examples of Phishing Threats

If you've ever interacted with crypto services publicly, such as on Bluesky, Twitter (now known as X), Instagram, or Facebook, you could be targeted by fake "wallet support" agents. Scammers employ bots that search for keywords like "Trust wallet issue," "Metamask support," "crypto recovery," and similar phrases, and target users with a barrage of fake support phishing attempts. As an exercise, I've posted messages on Twitter with those sorts of keywords and watched the messages roll in.

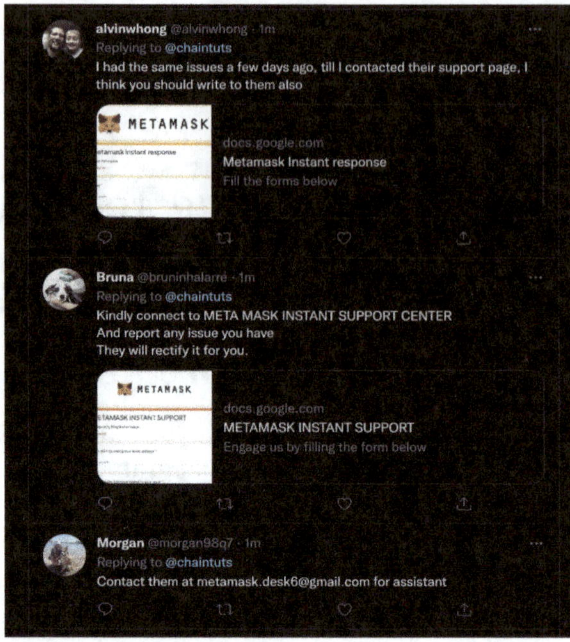

Wallet support phishing bots replying to an inquiry on Twitter

These messages all lead to Google Forms or email addresses asking for the same thing: my seed phrase. As we've discussed in previous chapters, the seed phrase is the piece of your personal cryptocurrency ecosystem that should be the most highly guarded, and *never* given to anyone else. Sadly though, this scam does work. If you're having trouble with your wallet or a transaction, a sophisticated phisher (who you presume has more technical expertise than you) can convince you that it's a technical necessity to share your phrase in order to diagnose and repair your issue. But no legitimate support line will ever ask for this information.

Data breaches also serve as a source for phishing targets. For example, the 2021 CoinMarketCap breach exposed the email addresses of some 3.1 million users. While having a public email in and of itself isn't a security hole like a password is, it can make you a target of phishing. My own email was exposed in this breach, and I have since received hundreds of cryptocurrency related phishing emails. Since the email was leaked from a cryptocurrency service, attackers assume you are likely (though not guaranteed) to use popular wallets and services. They send emails ranging from glaringly obvious to quite sophisticated, probing for weakness on the chance you'll give them private information like seed phrases.

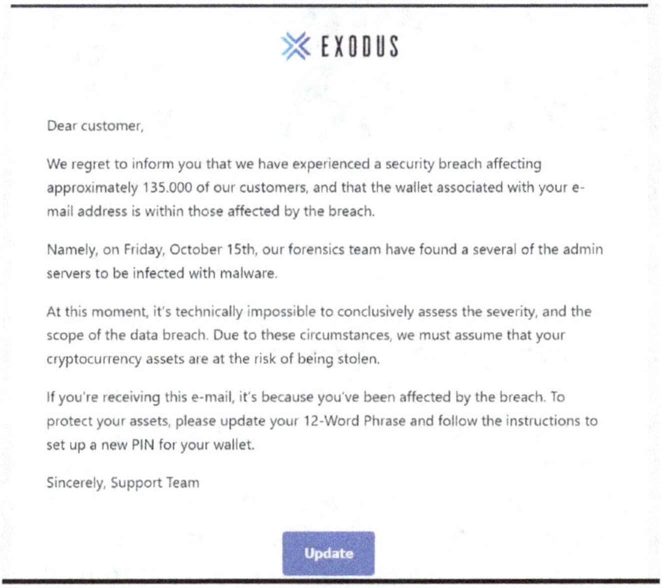

EXODUS

Dear customer,

We regret to inform you that we have experienced a security breach affecting approximately 135.000 of our customers, and that the wallet associated with your e-mail address is within those affected by the breach.

Namely, on Friday, October 15th, our forensics team have found a several of the admin servers to be infected with malware.

At this moment, it's technically impossible to conclusively assess the severity, and the scope of the data breach. Due to these circumstances, we must assume that your cryptocurrency assets are at the risk of being stolen.

If you're receiving this e-mail, it's because you've been affected by the breach. To protect your assets, please update your 12-Word Phrase and follow the instructions to set up a new PIN for your wallet.

Sincerely, Support Team

Update

A phishing email targeting users of Exodus wallet, asking for a 12 word seed phrase

Finally, you may encounter phishing simply by *searching* for wallet software. Attackers can use search engine optimization strategies to boost fake, but legitimate-looking websites in the search results. A search for "Keep Key Desktop", for example, yielded a website claiming to offer a web-based connection to a hardware wallet. Instead, what it really offered was a chance to input your seed phrase, giving the attackers access to the entire wallet of anyone who offered their keys.

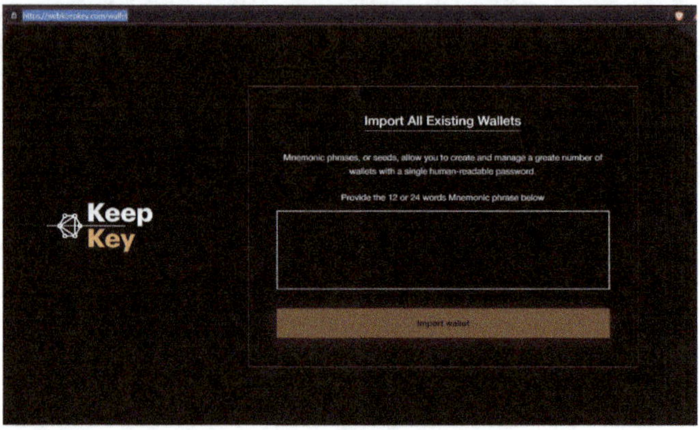

A phishing website pretending to be KeepKey wallet

Phishing scams often target seed phrases, as they are the most direct means for scammers to clean out a victim. Taking a seed phrase means instant access to that user's funds – the attacker can simply import the seed into a wallet and send the coins to their own wallet, an irreversible theft. However, attackers also target exchange accounts. Many users have large amounts of money stored in exchanges, and traditional phishing methods targeting passwords, 2FA, or device access are used to compromise those accounts.

Scammers may send emails with a link to fake login pages that collect the account password alongside the email or user ID. More sophisticated attacks such as fake support agent scams trick users into giving up 2FA codes, so that the account can be taken over *without* the password. By possessing a 2FA code, the attacker can initiate a password reset on the account, using the code as proof that they are the owner of the account (even though they are not). In some cases, these fake support agents may trick users into installing remote access software on their phone or PC, allowing them to open Authenticator apps or access stored passwords. This allows for easy account takeover.

Mitigation Strategies

Perhaps you believe that these examples are silly, and that no reasonably smart crypto user would fall for these schemes. But the reality is that many people do fall for them. That doesn't mean these victims aren't intelligent enough to spot phishing. Perhaps they were simply in a hurry, feeling threatened, or otherwise distracted before giving away their seed. If a user can't see their balance in a new wallet, they are more vulnerable to scams, especially if a fake "support agent" pretends to help but is actually looking to steal their seed phrase. Or perhaps a user is scared that their funds will be locked, as they don't yet understand that nobody can lock a user out of a non-custodial wallet.

Recognizing the patterns that phishers use can prevent you from becoming a victim. Educated users that take the time to think through what they are doing are the enemy of phishers, and those scared and in a rush are their friends.

One key mitigation strategy for phishing is to go directly to the target service, and never enter information by clicking on links or forms offered up by the email or other suspicious message. For example, if you receive an email claiming to be from Exodus wallet saying you'll be locked out, don't click on the link within that email. Instead, open up the Exodus wallet app on your phone directly. Check your balance – does anything actually appear to be off or missing? Are there any notifications within the app itself alerting you to a problem? If not, the email is likely to be phishing.

Another technique is to closely evaluate the source of the message. Many times, phishing emails don't even attempt to mask the true source. If you look at the "from" field of the email, you may see some random mailbox that makes no sense in this context. For example, an email supposedly from "Trust Wallet" that actually comes from emailshors@shorstravel.com.

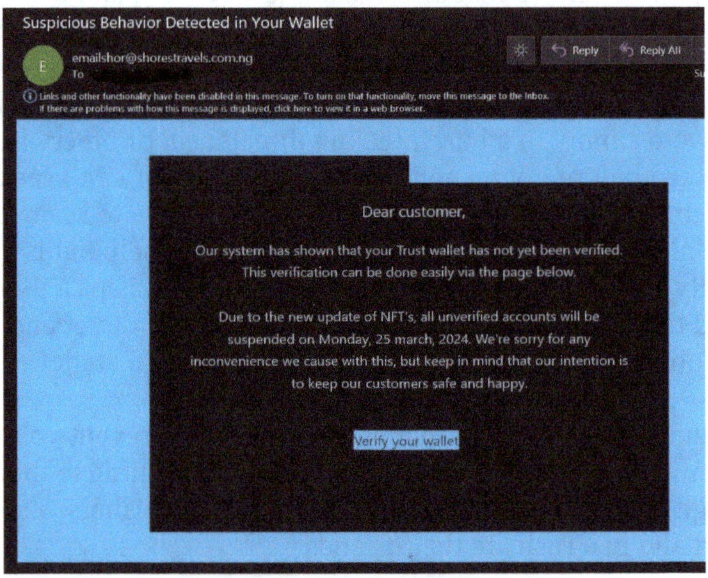

A Trust Wallet seed phrase phish with an obviously incorrect source

In this case, some unfortunate travel company's email service was compromised or *spoofed*, and the attackers made no attempt to hide the source. Sometimes, the from field can be spoofed by the attackers to match the expected account, so if something feels off you can view the actual email headers to see the real source. This is a bit more technical, but useful if you learn how to do so.

```
Received: from DIR-09 ([10.50.14.249])
          by localhost with LMTP
          id kCFLJibLaWalNzkA0J78UA
          (envelope-from <audreymathis@vaultoffer.info>)
          for [redacted]; Wed, 12 Jun 2024 12:21:58 -0400
```

Email headers from a phishing message showing the true source

Case Study: Fake Coinbase Support

A client contacted me that fell victim to a fraudulent Coinbase support scam. This person received a phone call claiming to be from Coinbase support, and the reason for the call is unknown. The victim was convinced to install a remote support app on their phone, and the agent gained access to 2FA codes. The attacker then reset the victim's password and took over the account.

Luckily, the victim in this case realized they were scammed and, with the assistance of a family member, locked their Coinbase account in time. No funds were lost, fortunately, and the victim was able to regain access to their account after some work with real Coinbase staff.

Lessons learned:

It's important to not immediately trust someone claiming to be support staff for an exchange or wallet. If you are suspicious, go directly to the website or wallet in question – in this case, coinbase.com. If you can log in and don't see any messages indicating a problem, your account is likely in good standing. *Never* give anyone access to a phone or PC via a remote support app – attackers can use this to steal 2FA codes, stored passwords, or even transfer themselves money directly from a wallet.

Case Study: Fraudulent Namecheap Support

I myself almost fell victim to a phishing scam. While not directly cryptocurrency related, this is a fine example of phishing scams, urgency, and mitigation techniques. I received an urgent warning that my Namecheap internet domain was expired. This meant (had the domain truly expired), that my users wouldn't have access to chaintuts content anymore! This email stated that I had to renew within 24 hours to keep my website available. This example led to a fake Namecheap login form, where the attackers could harvest my username and password!

Lessons learned:

I love this example in particular because I almost fell for it. Yes, phishing absolutely affects the cybersecurity aware too! I was in a hurry, and I thought that my Namecheap account had plenty of auto renewal funds. Nonetheless, I was alarmed and logged into my account to verify that my domains were, in fact, fine.

One particular mitigation technique saved me in that case. First of all, I knew that I had some time and that, to my recollection, my account was set up for auto renewal. So, something already felt off. This triggered my hesitancy to follow any links from the email itself. Instead of clicking the link in the email, I went *directly* to namecheap.com and checked. Had I clicked the link and entered my password into the fake form, I could have had my password compromised.

Another helpful tip that made me aware of this phishing scam was the *source* of the message. This isn't always easy. In this case, the attackers didn't even bother to change the "from" field of the email to match the purported source (something like support@namecheap.com). The email this came from was someone's (presumably compromised) business email. If the email "from" field had been spoofed, I could have viewed the email headers to verify the actual source.

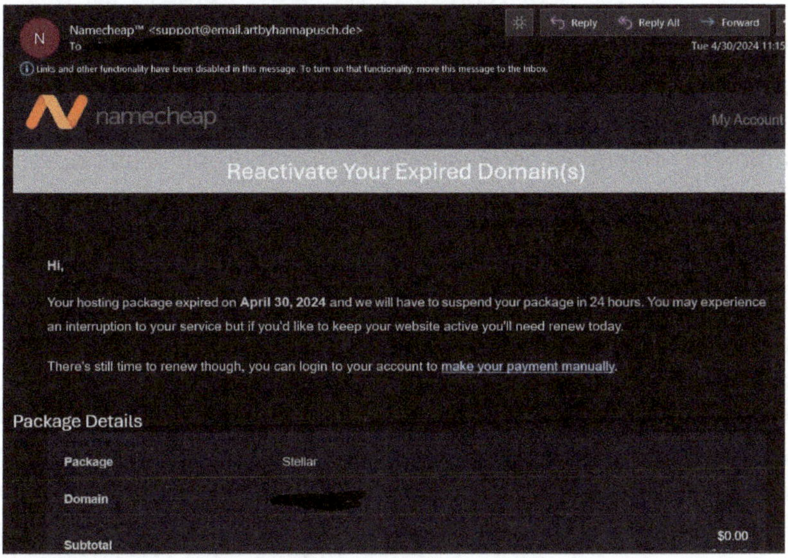

An urgent and fraudulent Namecheap domain expiration phish

Part 4, Chapter 4

Giveaway/Airdrop Phishing

One of the strong tactics that phishers use to steal cryptocurrency is enticing victims with the promise of a reward. Giveaway scams have been a part of the crypto landscape for quite some time, and have resulted in serious losses. These scams, similar to tech support scams, make use of some sense of authority – the scammers pretend to be someone they are not, but this time to offer rewards instead of technical assistance.

Airdrop scams often come with a similar type of impersonation – pretending to be a high profile company or person that's altruistically sending coins to users to "share the wealth." But really, they are about to steal from users. Some high-profile social media accounts from organizations such as the UFC (a mixed-martial arts promoter) have been compromised and used to conduct airdrop scams. Impersonating high-net-worth celebrities and others associated with the crypto space is relatively easy for scammers, and can reel in victims with a sense that these wealthy individuals might actually be doing charitable works. A sense of legitimacy is highly valuable for these attacks.

Examples of Phishing Threats

The first type of giveaway scam is the *crypto doubling* scam. With this attack, victims are told that if they send some amount of coins to an official "giveaway" address, they will receive double their money back. This is done under the auspices of "verifying" your wallet so they can send you the coins back. In reality, cryptocurrency transactions are irreversible. So, all you are doing is sending coins to the scammer's wallet, which they then keep for themselves. Attackers may use highly sophisticated and legitimate-looking websites, YouTube videos, or other resources to make the scam appear real.

A compromised UFC YouTube account using a high-net-worth celebrity's image for a crypto-doubling giveaway scam

The second type of airdrop scam worth mentioning is slightly more sophisticated than the doubling scam, which relies on users simply sending coins to an attacker-controlled address. Wallet drainers take advantage of the smart contract capabilities of blockchains such as Ethereum. With this scam, you're not asked to send coins directly to an address to get double your money back. Instead, you're asked to connect your wallet to receive the tokens. Using WalletConnect, your wallet can sign transactions in order to interact with smart contracts. In this case, you're signing a *malicious* contract that simply drains all available coins and tokens from that wallet.

Sometimes, these types of airdrop scams will also simply ask for a seed phrase as a way to “connect” your wallet. As we’ve discussed in previous chapters, the seed phrase grants access to all coins and tokens in a cryptocurrency wallet, and should never be shared under any circumstances. Attackers will often ask for the seed as a means to connect a wallet that doesn’t support WalletConnect for smart contracts. It’s just another way for them to ultimately drain your wallet.

A WalletConnect giveaway scam

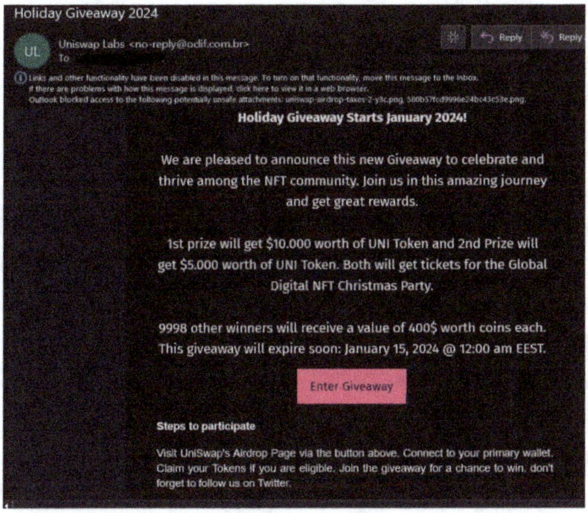

An email-based airdrop scam

Mitigation Strategies

Mitigating airdrop scams can be a bit more straightforward than sophisticated tech support scams, but again requires an awareness of the urgency the scammers want you to have. Most of these giveaway scams contain messages like “don’t be late,” or “hurry, this giveaway ends soon.” If you believe that you’ll miss a chance at free money, you’re more likely to act irrationally.

The tactic we can use to fight these scams is to evaluate if the reward is too good to be true. Does someone really want to send me $10,000 for free? Unlikely. As well, is that person likely to send out random emails to unexpected recipients? A legitimate giveaway won’t ask for private information or money in advance. In cryptocurrency, it’s especially important to think about the consequences. Never send money to get money, as transactions cannot be reversed. Never sign a random, unknown smart contract. In both cases, your money can be *irreversibly* lost. Take your time and act with rationality rather than greed.

Case Study: Crypto Doubling Scam

A client contacted me about crypto recovery after losing money to a giveaway scam. The victim was lured in by the promise of a giveaway from Chamath Palihapitiya, a well known venture capitalist and engineer. This scam promised to double the victim's bitcoin if they sent some amount to an address to verify their wallet. However, the victim never received any funds in return and realized this was a scam. Sadly, in this case, recovery was impossible and the victim lost roughly $5000 of bitcoin at the time.

Lessons Learned:

In this case the victim, an IT professional, was lured by the promise of reward from another admired technology professional, Chamath. Although this was not the *real* Chamath, the impersonation worked. It's always helpful to slow down and evaluate too-good-to-be-true rewards. It is difficult to write about such a loss, but it's important to understand that no matter our intelligence, professional skills, or awareness, all humans are vulnerable to social engineering tactics. I believe in this case that the victim may have avoided this loss by taking some extra time to evaluate the giveaway's legitimacy, but the message of "act now" by the scammers was too powerful.

A Chamath impersonator conducting a crypto doubling scam

Part 4, Chapter 5

Investment Scams

Investment scams, in my experience, tend to result in some of the biggest losses in the cryptocurrency space. These scams are also the most likely to hit those that aren't initially interested in Bitcoin or other technologies but are instead driven by the possibility of financial gains. Investment scams, as the name might suggest, are built on the fraudulent promise of returns if the victim is willing to send coins to the scammer as investment principal.

Often, these scams originate from cold contact on popular social media platforms. I've seen Instagram, LinkedIn, Twitter, and Bluesky used for investment scams with a fair amount of regularity. Wasting the time of these scammers often provides valuable information on how the scams actually play out. First, the attacker establishes a rapport with you, asking simple questions about where you're from, what you do for work, and what your hobbies are. They usually quickly move to the topic of "making passive income" by investing in cryptocurrency.

Examples of Investment Scams

The sophistication and length of these scams, sometimes called *pig butchering scams*, can vary. In some cases, a lone scammer impersonates a high-profile crypto celebrity and gives a deposit address to you via the chat. I've encountered several scammers pretending to be Andreas M. Antonopoulos or Roger Ver. This approach can lend some legitimacy to the scam, given that these figures are well-known experts in the cryptocurrency space.

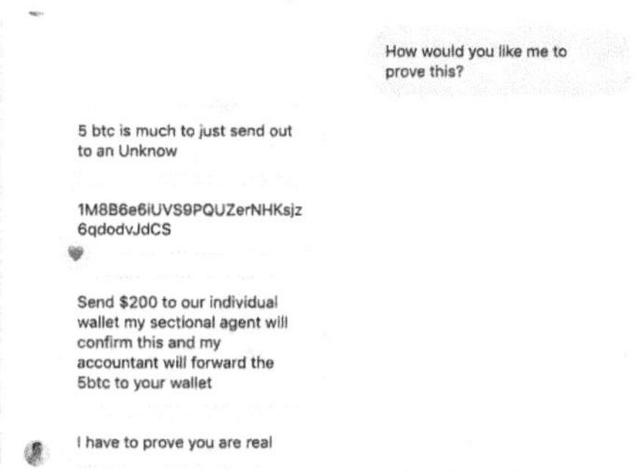

An Andreas impersonator asking for coins directly

In most cases, the scammer lures you to a fake but very convincing "investment platform." These websites, although showing signs of fraud to the trained eye, tend to look quite real. Within the site, you're prompted to set up an account and make your first deposit into the trading platform. This is where the theft takes place. You're not actually sending coins to a trading platform at all, you're simply sending into the wallet of the scammer. Once those coins are sent, there's no way to reverse the transaction to get your money back.

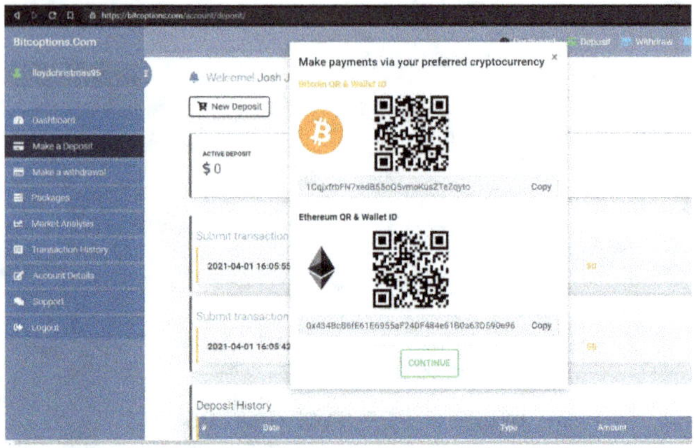

A legitimate, modern looking fake trading website

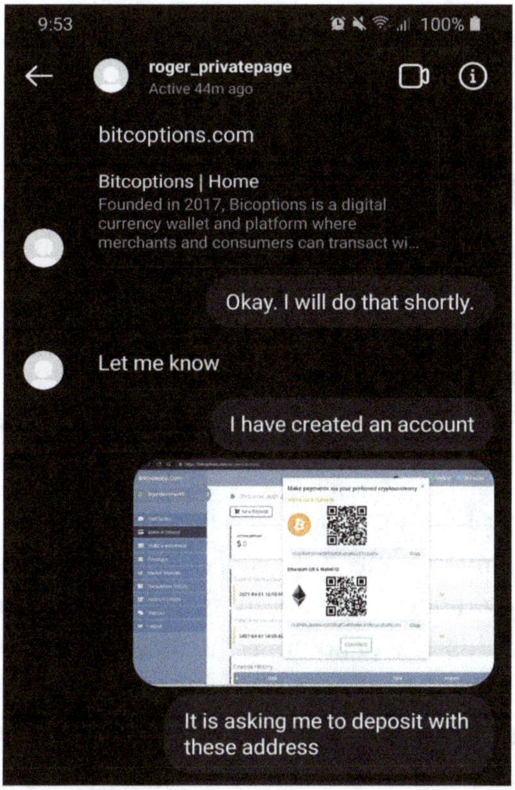

A Roger impersonator sending me to a fake trading website

These scams don't often stop at the first deposit, however. If the scammers know they've got you, they will try and extract as much money as possible from you before you catch on. Scammers will typically show "trading gains" via the fake website, making you *think* that the investment is paying off. One thing you'll never be able to do, however, is withdraw. The scammers will make up several excuses as to why you cannot get money back out of the platform; most often this reason is fake "taxes." The attacker will claim that you must pay taxes (in cryptocurrency, of course) before you can withdraw. This is nothing more than a final attempt to extract value from you before you realize that this is a scam.

Mitigation Steps

Investment scams are often difficult to mitigate, because they are multifaceted and tend to offer enticing rewards. What's worse is that overall, the rise of prices in the last ten years lends some legitimacy to the idea of "quick money" in crypto. However, there are several mitigation tactics we can use to avoid these scams in various stages.

First, be wary of cold-contact messages that immediately lead to talking about investments, especially if those investments are cryptocurrency related. The reality is that crypto is highly speculative at this time, and price fluctuations tend to keep legitimate financial planners away. Regardless, most legitimate investment professionals don't go right into recommending particular websites – they would instead schedule a call or an office visit. As well, be aware of impersonation – scammers often pretend to be a high-profile or high-net-worth crypto professional to gain your trust. But how likely is it that someone with a large following would contact you out-of-the-blue? Not very!

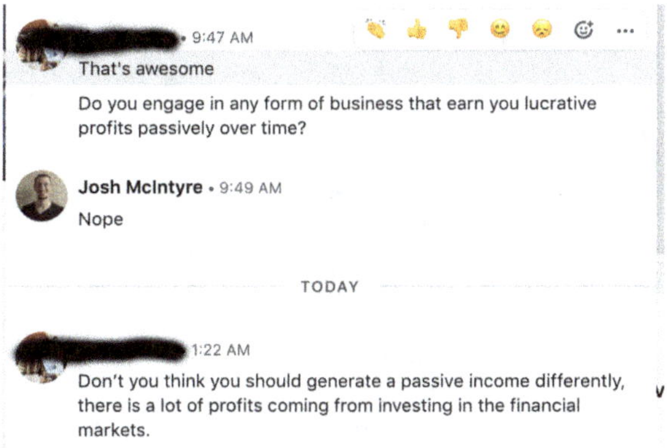

Cold contact messages discussing "passive income" are often a red flag

Next, take the time to evaluate a supposed investment website or business with a careful eye. Pig butchering scammers go to great lengths to make it appear that they are running a real business, but careful scrutiny can show why these websites and businesses are fraudulent. If you're technically savvy, using a whois tool can reveal how long a website has been available – a fake investment platform claiming to be 5 years old may have been registered for only a month, a clear red flag. As well, learn to spot fake business registrations or reviews. Scammers have even used pay-for-PR firms to publish news articles on their behalf, making it look as though this business has rave reviews.

tradingfxcore.com

Domain Information

Domain:	tradingfxcore.com
Registrar:	NameCheap, Inc.
Registered On:	2021-03-03
Expires On:	2022-03-03
Updated On:	2021-03-03
Status:	clientTransferProhibited
Name Servers:	dns1.namecheaphosting.com dns2.namecheaphosting.com

A whois tool showing a recently registered fake trading platform

```
josh@Josh-Asus:~$ whois aviorcapitalfinance.com
   Domain Name: AVIORCAPITALFINANCE.COM
   Registry Domain ID: 2516064148_DOMAIN_COM-VRSN
   Registrar WHOIS Server: whois.namecheap.com
   Registrar URL: http://www.namecheap.com
   Updated Date: 2020-04-18T11:27:38Z
   Creation Date: 2020-04-18T11:27:29Z
   Registry Expiry Date: 2021-04-18T11:27:29Z
   Registrar: NameCheap, Inc.
   Registrar IANA ID: 1068
   Registrar Abuse Contact Email: abuse@namecheap.com
   Registrar Abuse Contact Phone: +1.6613102107
   Domain Status: clientTransferProhibited https://icann.org/epp#clientTransferProhibited
   Name Server: DNS1.NAMECHEAPHOSTING.COM
   Name Server: DNS2.NAMECHEAPHOSTING.COM
   DNSSEC: unsigned
   URL of the ICANN Whois Inaccuracy Complaint Form: https://www.icann.org/wicf/
>>> Last update of whois database: 2020-12-01T17:44:21Z <<<
```

A command-line whois record of another fraudulent trading site

Finally, take the time to evaluate if the offered rewards are too-good-to-be-true. These websites often claim outlandish returns, sometimes 50-100% of your investment in a single day. No legitimate investment vehicle offers that type of return. In fact, many of these returns would have you earn more bitcoin than are in existence within a week or two of reinvesting your gains. Doing so would be completely impossible, making the fraudulent claims scary yet comical.

Too-good-to-be-true rates of return listed on a fake crypto investment website

Part 4, Chapter 6

Blackmail Scams

A typical blackmail scam starts something like this: you receive an email claiming that you have a "pending payment." This alone can grab your attention if you're not expecting it. But the scam quickly gets much worse – the scammer claims that they have gained total access to your device with malware! The scammer asserts control of your email, your webcam, your microphone, your files, and your contacts. And the scammer will leak embarrassing information about you to those contacts – unless you pay them in bitcoin.

This type of social engineering scam employs *fear*, a powerful tactic for exploiting people for money. Threats that take on a legal and social nature are remarkably effective when used for theft, and hackers employ several convincing tactics to make you feel like the threat is legitimate.

Examples of Blackmail Scams

The scammers often use an interesting trick to make you believe you've been compromised – they send the email from "your email." That is, they put your own email address in the "from" field of the email. If your email is x@y.com, the email states it is from x@y.com. This doesn't actually mean that this email was sent from your own mailbox – it just looks like it.

The scammers then get into the core of the scam – the threat and the demand for payment. Usually, the scammers claim to have used their malware to capture an embarrassing video of you, which they threaten to share with all of your friends, family, and coworkers.

The scammers demand payment in cryptocurrency – usually Bitcoin as it is the most popular and well known digital currency. The scammer claims that if you send payment to their Bitcoin address, they will delete the video and leave you alone.

Greetings!
Have you seen lately my e-mail to you from an account of yours?
Yeah, that merely confirms that I have gained a complete access to device of yours.

Within the past several months, I was observing you.
Are you still surprised how could that happen? Frankly speaking, malware has infected your devices and it's coming from an adult website, which you used to visit.
Although all this stuff may seem unfamiliar to you, but let me try to explain that to you.

With aid of Trojan Viruses, I managed to gain full access to any PC or other types of devices.
That merely means that I can watch you whenever I want via your screen just by activating your camera as well as microphone, while you don't even know about that.
Moreover, I have also received access to entire contacts list as well as full correspondence of yours.

A blackmail email specifically noting that it "came from your own email"

These scams can add further layers of threatening information to the emails, such as passwords leaked in previous data breaches. For example, perhaps you had a weak password “hunter2” for a website that suffered a breach. When the attackers cracked your password from that breach, it became publicly available in password dumps circulated around by malicious actors. Many people reuse passwords across websites and other services, and so there’s a likelihood you’re using that same password for your email account. You see your email password within the blackmail message, and *believe* your email has been compromised, even if it hasn’t.

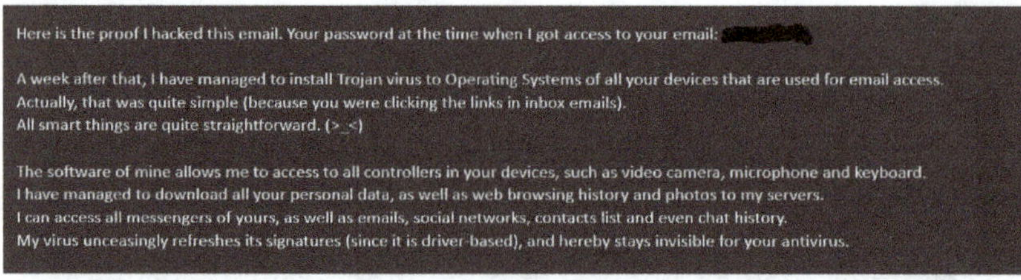

Here is the proof I hacked this email. Your password at the time when I got access to your email:

A week after that, I have managed to install Trojan virus to Operating Systems of all your devices that are used for email access.
Actually, that was quite simple (because you were clicking the links in inbox emails).
All smart things are quite straightforward. (>_<)

The software of mine allows me to access to all controllers in your devices, such as video camera, microphone and keyboard.
I have managed to download all your personal data, as well as web browsing history and photos to my servers.
I can access all messengers of yours, as well as emails, social networks, contacts list and even chat history.
My virus unceasingly refreshes its signatures (since it is driver-based), and hereby stays invisible for your antivirus.

A blackmail message with a password from a previous data breach

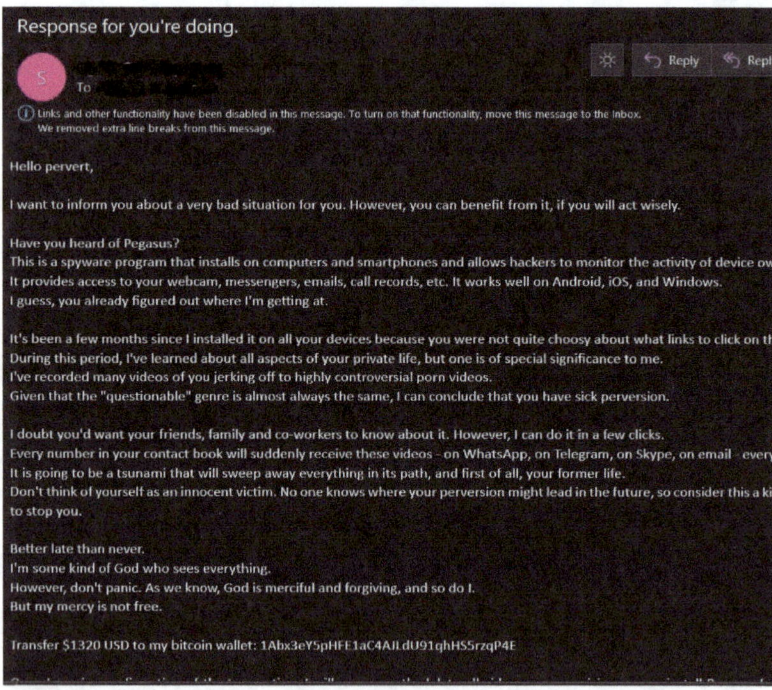

Response for you're doing.

S

To

Reply Reply

Links and other functionality have been disabled in this message. To turn on that functionality, move this message to the Inbox.
We removed extra line breaks from this message.

Hello pervert,

I want to inform you about a very bad situation for you. However, you can benefit from it, if you will act wisely.

Have you heard of Pegasus?
This is a spyware program that installs on computers and smartphones and allows hackers to monitor the activity of device owr
It provides access to your webcam, messengers, emails, call records, etc. It works well on Android, iOS, and Windows.
I guess, you already figured out where I'm getting at.

It's been a few months since I installed it on all your devices because you were not quite choosy about what links to click on the
During this period, I've learned about all aspects of your private life, but one is of special significance to me.
I've recorded many videos of you jerking off to highly controversial porn videos.
Given that the "questionable" genre is almost always the same, I can conclude that you have sick perversion.

I doubt you'd want your friends, family and co-workers to know about it. However, I can do it in a few clicks.
Every number in your contact book will suddenly receive these videos - on WhatsApp, on Telegram, on Skype, on email - every
It is going to be a tsunami that will sweep away everything in its path, and first of all, your former life.
Don't think of yourself as an innocent victim. No one knows where your perversion might lead in the future, so consider this a kin
to stop you.

Better late than never.
I'm some kind of God who sees everything.
However, don't panic. As we know, God is merciful and forgiving, and so do I.
But my mercy is not free.

Transfer $1320 USD to my bitcoin wallet: 1Abx3eY5pHFE1aC4AJLdU91qhHS5rzqP4E

A blackmail message with threats and a Bitcoin address

Mitigation Steps

With the email "from" trick and leaked passwords, these blackmail messages can be pretty threatening. In this case, it is important to both slow down and evaluate the threat. It’s pretty unlikely that this attacker actually has full access to your computer. Modern operating systems and antivirus software are pretty good, and malware proliferation doesn’t usually happen through most of the legitimate websites you visit. This is not a foolproof assumption, as this type of spyware does exist. It just isn't that likely that you've acquired it on your system through normal use. Second, you may not do the embarrassing thing that the hacker is threatening you with in the first place.

Even if an attacker did have full access to your PC, your browsing habits, and your contacts, they probably aren’t going to threaten you and ask for a relative pittance in Bitcoin. It would be easier, more efficient, and more discreet to just steal your passwords for bank accounts, cryptocurrency exchanges, or wallets and then steal everything they can that way. Why bother asking you? In this case, they’re asking because they don’t actually have any access to your system at all. They just sent an email (which anyone can do) hoping you’ll panic and send them an irreversible form of payment.

Since scammers don’t actually have anything damaging to you, they simply send you an email with a threat. Remember, anyone can send an email to anyone. And anyone can set the “from” field of an email to anything they want. Scammers rely on fear and time pressure, both of which are classic social engineering tactics. They hope you’ll be scared enough to send them cryptocurrency, which is an irreversible form of payment. However, you don’t have to send them anything! They don’t truly have access to your email, your device, or any private information about you. It’s all a trick using simple mass email tools and social engineering.

Part 4, Chapter 7

Recovery Scams

All of the scams we've discussed so far cover the wide variety of ways an attacker may try to steal cryptocurrency from you – such as investment scams, fake wallets, fraudulent services, malicious airdrops, and blackmail. All result in a loss of cryptocurrency, whether through gaining access to your wallet keys, signing a wallet-draining contract, or directly transacting with a scammer who tricked you via social engineering. The last type of scam we'll discuss is one that can occur after you have already been victimized by one of these other attacks. This is the fake *recovery* scam.

After a loss, many users are desperate to try and recover some of their stolen funds. It hurts to lose money, and the fact that the loss occurred due to social engineering could make them feel embarrassed, unintelligent, and desperate to repair the loss. Even though the smartest folks can fall victim to a scam, sophisticated attackers use embarrassment and desperation to their advantage to steal from you again – this time by convincing you to use a fake recovery service. In nearly all cases, it's not technically possible to recover lost or stolen coins due to the nature of cryptocurrency transactions. Yet, attackers will convince you that they have some special "hacking knowledge" to get your money back, and in the process, steal even more money.

Examples of Recovery Scams

Recovery scammers can advertise their fraudulent services in a myriad of ways, but social media is a useful tool for reaching a wide audience of potential targets. If you've ever mentioned keywords like "crypto," "bitcoin," "wallet," or "recovery" in a comment, you may have seen bot replies advertising the services of a professional "hacker."

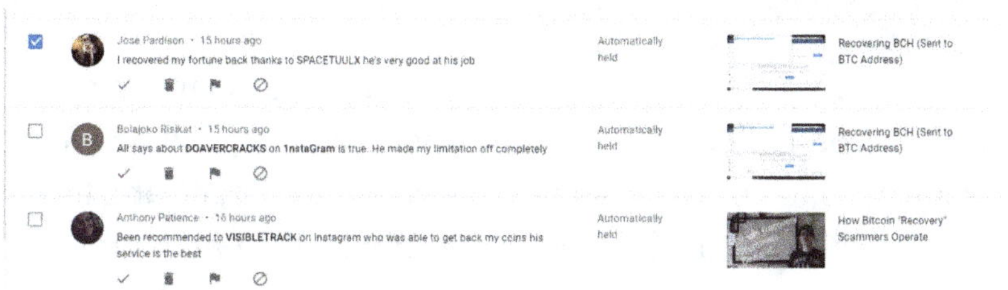

Bot comments advertising fake recovery services

These fake services tend to operate on common social media platforms such as Instagram, where targets are readily available and it's easy to create new accounts once the old ones are reported or deleted. Similar to other scams, attackers sometimes use impersonation – pretending to be a respected figure in the crypto community. I've even seen myself impersonated in my own comment section, which is both jarring and hilarious.

A chaintuts impersonator luring potential victims to WhatsApp

Once a recovery scammer has made contact, they can attempt to steal from you in several ways. The first, simplest, and perhaps easiest way is to convince you that they are legitimate and to ask you to pay upfront for services. For example, they may say that their upfront deposit for recovery is $150 in Bitcoin. Once you pay, they can take that money and run, with no way for you to conduct a chargeback.

But once you're on the hook, the scammers want to extract as much as possible from you. So, they will usually trick you into giving up access to other wallets or exchange accounts in order to empty them out. In one interaction with a recovery scammer, I was asked to provide 2FA codes for a Coinbase account. These codes could be used to conduct a password reset and steal my account without me giving up my password. By using clever technical language, a scammer may convince you this is safe since you don't have to give a password. Most people are aware that giving a password to someone else is risky. But 2FA codes in the hands of an attacker can be just as dangerous.

Attackers are also likely to ask for a seed phrase if a self-custody wallet was involved in the initial loss. Seed phrases grant access to all of the coins and tokens in a wallet, and so the scammer wants them as an easy means to clean out your account. Seed phrases or individual private keys are a high value target that should *never* be shared with anyone, let alone a stranger.

Recognizing this part of the scam can actually be difficult, as there are some very rare cases where a seed phrase can be used to recover misplaced coins in your own wallets – for example, if you sent Bitcoin Cash or another Bitcoin fork to a Bitcoin address in your own self-custody wallet. In those cases though, a legitimate helper would likely guide you through those steps yourself, rather than asking for the seed. In my consulting experience, I guide users through their own recoveries as this is the most secure avenue for handling these cases.

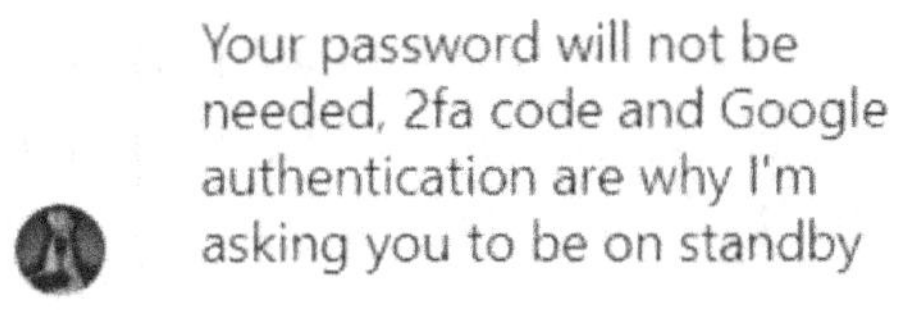

A recovery scammer asking for Coinbase 2FA codes

The same scammer requesting an upfront payment in Bitcoin

Case Study

A chaintuts viewer on YouTube commented on a video in the midst of a recovery scam. The fraudulent hacker asked them to use CashApp, a custodial service for Bitcoin. The attacker tried to trick them into enabling on-chain transactions, a feature that would allow the scammer to send any of the user's available balance to their own Bitcoin wallet. I replied to this comment advising the user not to do this, to immediately cut off contact with the scammer, and to change any relevant password and 2FA settings immediately. Thankfully, this user reported that they stopped before the attacker was able to send out coins, but it was a close call.

Lessons Learned:

The attacker was so adamant about enabling on-chain transactions because this would allow them to send themselves coins in an irreversible way. Once a transaction was sent on the Bitcoin blockchain, the attacker would have full access to the coins with no chargeback mechanism available to the user. It's possible that a CashApp-to-CashApp user transaction – which actually occurs in a centralized database rather than on the blockchain – could be reversed – but certainly not a real Bitcoin transaction.

Never allow anyone access to your accounts, even if they claim it's for recovery purposes. Someone with access to your exchange accounts could change settings, clean out your accounts, or set you up for future compromise.

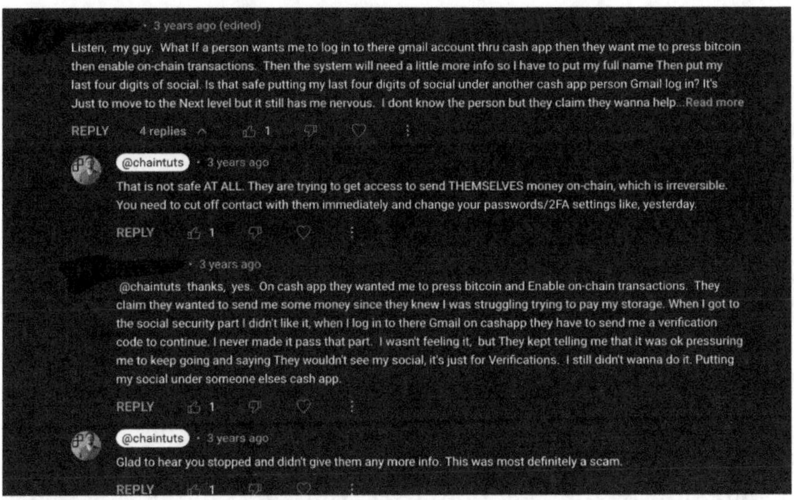

A chaintuts viewer almost caught in a recovery scam, asking for Bitcoin via CashApp

Part 4, Chapter 8

Malware Threats

Much of what we have covered so far involves social engineering, various forms of phishing that threaten user funds. People are often easier to break than systems. It's usually an easier route to financial reward to trick a user into giving up their seed phrase voluntarily than it is to steal it through some sort of technical means. That doesn't mean such avenues don't exist, though. Technical exploits of varying levels of sophistication and effectiveness work to steal user's coins. One such avenue, *malware*, will be familiar to computer users of all levels of knowledge.

Malware, or malicious software, can find its way on to the PCs of cryptocurrency users and threaten their coins through different exploits. Here, we're not going to cover all the possible forms of malware or how they get onto user computers in the first place. Instead, we'll discuss a few methods of attack that virus authors use to steal cryptocurrency from victims. In particular, address-swapping attacks and seed-stealing or key-stealing malware threats. Both attacks involve relatively simple methodologies, and are quick ways for your coins to disappear from your wallet.

Address-Swapping Malware

One malware attack on crypto users takes advantage of the complexity of public addresses. Cryptocurrency addresses for networks such as Bitcoin and Ethereum are long, complex, random strings. A legacy Bitcoin address, for example, is 34+ characters of base58 encoded data, containing select upper and lowercase letters plus numbers. Ethereum uses 42 character addresses of hexadecimal – characters 0-9 and a-f. These strings are difficult to remember and transcribe when creating transactions, so most users will scan QR codes or use the copy-paste function of a PC.

Most users on a PC will simply highlight the address of their intended recipient, right click, and copy the address to the operating system's clipboard. They will then navigate to the sending wallet and paste the address in the destination field. Many don't double check that the address pasted correctly, or that it is the same address that they originally copied. And that is precisely what *address-swapping* malware takes advantage of.

This type of malware is relatively simple in its construction. Once on a user's machine, this software polls the clipboard, the OS construct that allows a user to copy-paste information. When there's a string in the clipboard, the malware scans it and determines if it matches the pattern of a cryptocurrency address. If there's a match, the code replaces the user's intended address with that of the attacker's. When the user pastes the address and doesn't double check it, they send coins to the attacker's wallet instead of their intended recipient.

For example, let's say a user copies a Bitcoin address starting with 167pV6Un and so on. The malware detects this address in the clipboard using pattern matching code called a *regular expression*. The malware then finds a similar Bitcoin address in its database and replaces the original in the clipboard. The attacker address, starting with 1673Hje7, is pasted by the user.

They assume the pasted address is the correct one, and complete the transaction. Now the coins belong to the malware authors, not the intended recipient. Blockchain transactions are irreversible, so there's no way for the victim to get that money back.

Example user address swap

`167pV6UnXfYe6DFyxubM45rWVeW1uA6bF7` →

`1673Hje7kdTtTmbT7GWmdWJyUDwjE8ZYCg`

A simple demo of this functionality can be coded quickly, using common programming languages and libraries. More sophisticated forms of this malware will often generate attacker addresses that start with the same few characters as those of the victim's. In our previous example, both the victim address and the attacker address start with the characters 167. Depending on the available resources and internal workings of the malware, attackers may try to match even more characters. The more characters the attacker wishes to match, the more computing power it takes to generate possible addresses – so it's usually only a small handful. If you're not being careful, and the first three or four characters match, the modified address is likely to sneak past you without raising suspicion – especially if you're in a hurry.

There's also the tangentially related attack called *address poisoning*. For this attack, hackers send very small transactions to public addresses on the blockchain, transferring fractions of a penny. This means that in your wallet, the attacker address will show up in your transaction history. If you're not careful, you may copy this address to your clipboard thinking it's the address of a previous transaction from your own wallet. When you paste this address, you're inadvertently sending the coins to the attacker instead of your intended recipient.

Preventing this sort of malware or poisoning attack is twofold. First, of course, you should strive to keep your systems free of malware in the first place. Keeping your PC up-to-date and using antivirus software will prevent this kind of malicious code from running in the first place. You should take special care with systems you frequently use to execute cryptocurrency transactions or store keys on.

Second, it's possible to prevent this attack even on an infected system, by *always* double and triple checking your addresses before you send a transaction. This is a good practice irrespective of malware infections – this can also prevent a simple mistake from turning into an irreversible disaster. Always double check that the address you are sending to exactly matches the one you intend.

Check where you got the address from. Make sure it's the right recipient wallet. Check that the address is complete and matches the cryptocurrency you intend to use. Ensure you're using a BTC address for BTC transactions, LTC for LTC, ETH for ETH. Many blockchains share an address format, or use addresses that are similar enough that wallets will accept the "wrong" address as technically valid. Finally, check that all the characters match. Given how cryptographic hashes work, it's usually sufficient to check the first and last 10 characters or so for small transactions. For particularly high value transactions, you may wish to check that *all* characters match, even if it's a bit time consuming.

Remember that blockchain transactions are irreversible once sent, so take the extra time to validate your addresses before hitting send. An extra ten seconds of validation can save you from significant loss if address-swapping malware makes its way onto your system.

Case Study

A client reached out for help concerning an Ethereum transaction gone astray. This user had intended to send ETH to another wallet, completed the transaction, and found that the funds did not turn up where they should have. Upon further inspection, this user realized that the Ethereum address did not belong to their intended recipient and appeared totally random to them. I discussed crypto address-swapping malware with the user, and they ran a malware scan on their PC using common free software. The user frequented file-sharing websites (using torrents) and discovered a plethora of malware on their system using the scanner. It appears that crypto address-swapping malware was the source of the trouble, and this user lost their money.

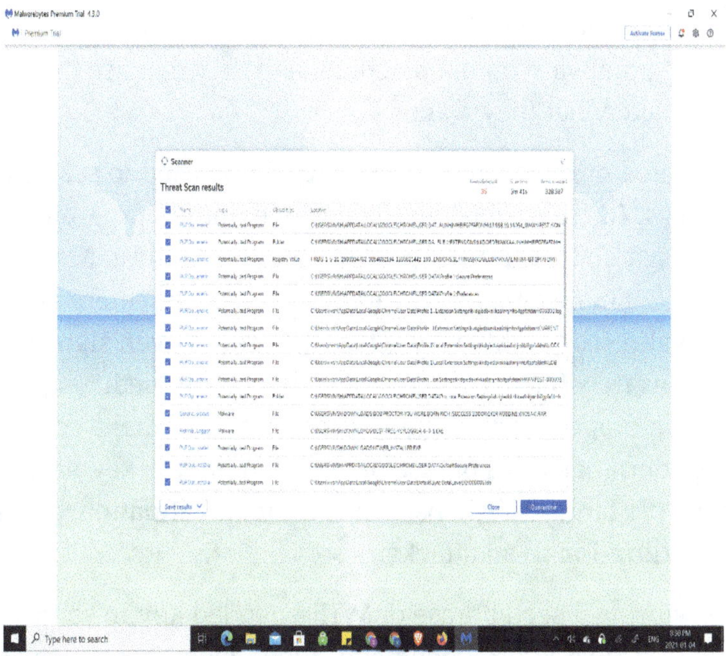

The highly infected Windows system of a crypto address-swapping malware victim

Seed-Stealing or Key-Stealing Malware

A second form of crypto-theft malware doesn't rely as much on user carelessness as address-swapping variants do. This type of malware goes directly after the bank vault – the user's private keys themselves. Seed-stealing or key-stealing malware leverages privileged access to the user's machine to steal keys and use them to sign transactions, thus permanently taking the victim's coins without relying on social engineering or waiting for a user to miscopy an address. This type of attack is probably the greatest malware threat to crypto assets, because it requires no user interaction or mistakes. All an attacker needs is the initial mistake of allowing malware onto a machine, and they can use this deep access to take what they want.

Sophisticated or even simple malware can be used to scan for crypto keys. It's relatively simple to use common programming tools and search files for the pattern of a seed phrase. More sophisticated malware could search files for that pattern and verify a valid seed right away. This code could even sign transactions transferring coins to the attacker immediately. Any plain-text storage of cryptographic key data will make scanning for the pattern of a seed phrase or encoded private key easy for software. It's largely basic pattern matching, validation, and some sort of exfiltration to an attacker's server.

Beyond storing a seed phrase or WIF-encoded key in some sort of text file (.txt files, Word documents, Open Document Format, and the like), it's even possible for seed-scanning to occur via things like screenshots or pictures of seeds. Optical Character Recognition (OCR) could be used to scan for seed words in a user's image files, using similar pattern matching to that of plain-text file attacks. Or, malware could simply take periodic screenshots of a target machine and the attacker could look for seeds manually.

For this reason, it's absolutely critical to never store a cryptocurrency seed phrase or private key in any plaintext form. By plaintext, I don't simply mean "in a text document," but rather, *unencrypted.* Storing the seed phrase for a hot wallet in an *encrypted* form on a PC is reasonable, since the wallet itself stores an encrypted copy of the keys already. You don't necessarily gain or lose much in the way of security by storing a backup of your hot wallet seed in a secure password manager, for example. Of course, this means you must protect that encrypted vault with a long, strong passphrase that's resistant to cracking in case some form of malware manages to steal the vault itself. This digital backup does present a second attack vector, but balances that concern with the convenience.

It's certainly possible for this type of malware to steal files that likely contain encrypted keys, such as a *wallet.dat* file. In this case, the attacker could not immediately steal the coins, but would have to run password cracking operations to try and decrypt that file. This is why it is so important to protect your wallets, password managers, and other resources with strong, high entropy passphrases.

In any case, having crypto-attacking malware on your system is very bad news. If there's malicious software running on your system, there's so many possible avenues of attack that it's very likely you'll be compromised in some way. Prevention is the best policy – keep your system and antivirus software up to date and free of known vulnerabilities as much as possible. Be mindful of the software you download and install on your machine. Don't install software from untrusted sources and be wary of any website asking you to install something. It's best to stick with well known, well vetted, or even open-source code for your wallets. If a website or giveaway is asking you to install something with the promise of a reward, it's very likely a scam trying to trick you into installing malware. Caution is key, because malware threats can clean out your wallet in minutes or even seconds.

Part 4, Chapter 9

Mistakes to Watch For

When most of us think of threats to our digital assets, we think of external threats – in other words, someone else trying to steal our coins. But we don't often realize that another threat to the security of those assets is ourselves. *Mistakes* can also quickly and easily lose us our coins. Mistakes can be particularly difficult to guard against, because as individuals we are biased. We think that we are smart enough to not make mistakes, when in reality, such errors are easy to make for anyone.

Awareness and vigilance for common crypto mistakes can help us increase our security and defeat this bias. By taking the time to be aware of common errors in handling our keys and transactions, we can reduce the chances of creating our own downfall. Mistakes in cryptocurrency are often completely irreversible, so stopping them before they happen is the only means of protection. The two biggest problems to look out for are key loss and cross-chain address swaps.

Key Loss

The worst user error one can make with cryptocurrency is also the simplest to understand, and the simplest to mitigate. Recall from previous chapters that we must retain backups of our crypto keys if using a non-custodial wallet. Key loss is a threat to our assets that's self-induced, where we simply misplace, destroy, or otherwise lose access to our seed phrase or private keys. This one's pretty obvious, and it might seem like it's not worth dedicating a few extra paragraphs to after several chapters on key backups and non-custodial security. But here, it's worth a reminder that backup loss is actively a threat to the security of your digital assets.

You can follow all of the best practices for a hardware wallet – generate a strong device PIN, engrave the seed in metal, and make multiple backups. You can never put the seed on a computer, ever. But say that before you spread your backups to multiple locations, you toss them in a drawer and promptly forget about them. Maybe you inadvertently toss the metal seeds in a cleaning frenzy, forgetting what they were. Or maybe you throw the paper seeds in a drawer and accidentally spill your hydrating liquid of choice down the desk, rendering them unreadable. In a further spate of bad luck, your hardware device crashes, and you are simply out of luck. Without your seed, there's no way to recover or access potentially thousands of dollars' worth of digital assets permanently.

All of the best security practices are worth little if you don't practice mindfulness around maintaining those solid backups, including awareness of where they are and how to use them. It's worth explicitly taking time to think about your plan, so that accidental key loss isn't a factor. Make your backups, and actively ensure you know where they are and how to get to them at all times. Periodically check that they are intact and readable. Consider the possibility of contamination, such as spills, and protect against those concerns. A backup isn't a backup unless it's tested, and so taking the time to think about your plan can save you from headaches when you really need it. It can be as simple as saying to yourself, "OK, my hardware wallet is stored here, my primary seed backup is in the safe, and my other backup is in the safety deposit box at the bank." You could even write this down as a note for yourself and your heirs in the event of an emergency. Just don't set your backup down <somewhere>, forget about it, and end up in a key loss situation.

Cross-Chain Address Swaps

Another more insidious mistake is *cross-chain address swapping.* In other words, sending coins to an address from the wrong cryptocurrency. This mistake is often possible because many popular coins share an address format, and therefore a set of valid addresses a user can send to. Let's say for example you wish to send Bitcoin Cash (BCH) to a friend. Your friend is using a wallet that supports both Bitcoin Cash (BCH) and Bitcoin (BTC). Your friend inadvertently copies a BTC address and gives it to you. You send the transaction to that address, and much to your mutual dismay, the BCH never shows up in your friend's wallet!

When you broadcast this transaction, it is processed entirely by the Bitcoin Cash (BCH) network. Even though this user's address came from their Bitcoin (BTC) wallet, nothing happens on the Bitcoin chain because these are two entirely different systems. The issue here is that the coins share a legacy address format, with base58check addresses that start with a 1. The Bitcoin Cash wallet accepts the BTC address as valid, because it is indeed a valid BCH address. The problem here is that the receiving user's wallet isn't looking for BCH at that address, since it came from the BTC derivation path. This can often happen with Ethereum and Ethereum-based tokens as well, since they share the same hexadecimal-based address format.

In some cases, it's possible to recover the coins if the receiver has the seed phrase for a non-custodial wallet, and the address format doesn't have compatibility issues. If you send BCH to a BTC legacy address (starting with a 1), and the user has a seed phrase for the wallet, you can manually retrieve the coins. You can do so by finding the individual private key for the address using a BIP39/BIP44 tool, and importing that key into a Bitcoin Cash wallet. The same can be true for Ethereum-based coins and tokens for wallets that use BIP39 and BIP44 standards.

This process is often impossible, however. With BTC and BCH swaps, the segwit address format commonly used by BTC wallets is not supported by the BCH protocol. Segwit is a protocol addition specific to Bitcoin designed for scalability and second-layer technologies. Unfortunately, the actual address characters themselves are considered valid as a BCH multisig address. Multisignature technology requires multiple signing keys to produce a valid transaction. It just so happens that multisig and segwit addresses share the same format. This means in practical terms that your BCH wallet will allow you to send coins to a BTC segwit address, but the coins will be unrecoverable once the transaction is complete.

Another complication occurs when this mistake happens using a custodial wallet. If you send coins to the wrong address and the receiver is an exchange or other custodial service, they'll never credit the coins to the proper account. Exchange support personnel do not have access to the private keys needed for a recovery for security reasons. As well, the process is tedious, error prone, and a security risk. So, in 99% of cases, if you send coins to the wrong wallet address at an exchange, those coins will be permanently lost. There have even been cases where exchange addresses "expire", so that a user sending to a previous address in their transaction history would not have those coins credited to their account.

Prevention in this case is similar to the prevention used for address-swapping malware attacks. Always double, triple check your address before sending coins. Verify *explicitly* with the recipient that the address is for the right cryptocurrency before you send your transaction. For example, ensure that your friend copies a Bitcoin Cash address for a Bitcoin Cash transaction, and that it isn't a Bitcoin address. Be especially mindful of format issues like segwit – addresses that start with a 3. If your friend gives you a BCH address that starts with a 3, this should be a red flag to stop and double check. If your friend is sophisticated enough to use a 3 multisig address for BCH, they should be able to confirm this detail with you. In most cases it's a simple mistake where a user copies a BTC segwit address instead.

When possible, use address formats that are specific to only one cryptocurrency. Due to frequent mistakes like the one described here, Bitcoin Cash adopted the *CashAddr* format, specific to BCH only. Addresses usually start with a q. This format looks entirely different from BTC's base58check format, so it's obvious it belongs to the correct currency. BTC adopted the bech32 format, starting with bc1, for similar reasons. By using these formats where possible, you can avoid cross-chain address-swap mistakes.

Remember that cryptocurrency transactions are irreversible once sent, and only in some rare cases is a recovery possible. It's best to always double, triple check the address and currency before broadcasting a transaction. Prevention is the key and avoids costly mistakes. We're often in a hurry and get comfortable, so make it a habit to check your transactions every single time. Don't assume that you're too smart to make a mistake, because we're all vulnerable to such errors – especially when experience turns to complacency.

Part 4, Chapter 10

Security Review

Digital asset ownership is certainly more involved than traditional finance. With the power of self-sovereign money comes a greater responsibility for users and a requirement that they take security into their own hands. Thankfully, we've learned a myriad of techniques for understanding security throughout this book.

First, we've covered the basics of asset ownership with private key formats and control models. The differences between self-custody and managed-custody solutions inform the security approach we must take. Ultimately, private keys are the core of crypto ownership, and guarding those keys is the core of security. For exchange accounts, we trust a custodian to manage the keys for us – trading off convenience and, hopefully, expertise for the price of reduced self-sovereignty. This approach requires a more traditional form of security that is applied to our online accounts. Managing passwords, 2FA, and email hygiene keeps us safe in that regard.

For self-sovereign crypto management, we can use various forms of non-custodial wallets. Hot wallets give us the flexibility of everyday spending, and the ability to run full nodes and support the network. These wallets, while somewhat vulnerable to attack, offer a reasonable level of security for everyday use. Hardware or cold wallets are the pinnacle of security for most users; specialized devices that keep your keys safe offline and sign transactions away from prying eyes. Whichever wallet type we choose, proper key backups protect us from the loss of the original, and are hardened against fire, flood, and forgetfulness.

Finally, we've reviewed the many possible threats that seek to steal your coins. Social engineering remains one of the most common avenues of attack, since it's easier to trick someone than to compromise systems in many cases. Next, we've covered malware threats that seek your keys and coins by compromising the software on your PC. And finally, we've discussed mistakes – the ways we can lose our own keys due to carelessness or simple human nature.

This book has covered a wide variety of security recommendations for all of the most common types of crypto wallets, from exchanges to hardware. I hope that you've walked away with not only a set of practices, but a deeper understanding of why these practices are designed in the first place. Knowledge of the principles of security will help you put these guidelines into practice, with a keen eye towards your own risks and needs. The cryptocurrency landscape, like that of most technology, is evolving rapidly. New methods of attack are being invented, and mitigation steps just behind them. This book is a general guide to understanding and implementing crypto asset security, but can't cover every possible scenario. It's up to you to learn from many sources and stay up-to-date as the space evolves. With the proper training, all of us can stay aware and help develop sound security hygiene. Maintaining our own digital sovereignty is key in this fascinating and powerful world of cryptocurrency technology.

About the Author

Josh McIntyre is a professional software engineer and technical educator with a passion for cryptocurrency technology and teaching others. With his project chaintuts, he creates free and open license tech education content centering around cryptocurrencies, cybersecurity, and computer science. When not working with technology, Josh is an avid active adventurer. He enjoys spending time with his wife Maria and their pets.

www.ingramcontent.com/pod-product-compliance
Lightning Source LLC
LaVergne TN
LVHW022050200926
848481LV00003B/854